NEW EDITION

LIFESAVER

Basic English in Medical Situations

Maki Inoue   Toshiya Sato

JN209066

NATIONAL GEOGRAPHIC LEARNING

Australia • Brazil • Mexico • Singapore • United Kingdom • United States

NATIONAL GEOGRAPHIC
LEARNING

Lifesaver, New Edition—Basic English in Medical Situations

Maki Inoue / Toshiya Sato

Text credits appear on page 126, which constitutes a continuation of the copyright page.

Photo Credits:
Cover: © Manfred Ruts/Getty Images
p. 33: © iStock.com/bee32; p. 52: © iStock.com/Portugal2004; p. 68: © PPS Digital Network (RM)/ Pacific Press Service; p. 76: © iStock.com/Yuki KONDO; p. 108: © iStock.com/sturui; p. 125: © MSF

ISBN: 978-4-86312-366-3

National Geographic Learning | Cengage Learning K.K.
No. 2 Funato Building 5th Floor
1-11-11 Kudankita, Chiyoda-ku
Tokyo 102-0073
Japan

Tel: 03-3511-4392
Fax: 03-3511-4391

Contents

はじめに

Lifesaver が生まれ変わりました！日進月歩で変化していく医療現場のニーズに合わせて、より新しく、より興味深く、より臨床現場に寄り添った内容を心がけて改訂しました。

今日、日本には250万人以上の外国人が暮らしています。彼らは日常生活の中で、言葉が通じないせいで不自由を感じたり、嫌な思いをしたり、不安を抱えたりすることがあります。外国人患者が以前より多く訪れる病院では、医療従事者は彼らとなかなか思うようにコミュニケーションがとれません。日本もグローバル化の波を大きく受けていることを考えると、医療従事者は、病院を訪れる患者に、日本人であろうと外国人であろうと同じ質のケアを与えることが望まれており、そのためにはコミュニケーションをとるための基本的な英語力をつける必要があります。

本書は、このような時代の要求に合った、医療現場で本当に必要な英語表現や専門用語を身につけることを目的に作られました。忙しいカリキュラムの勉強をこなしながらも、将来プロの看護師になる夢を抱いて前向きに取り組む学生たちに、看護の現場で本当に役に立つ英語表現を学んでほしいと思います。外国人患者と英語でコミュニケーションがとれたときの喜びを経験して、より満足のいく看護ができたという充実感を味わってください。

この改訂版では、より良い本にするために以下の4点を考慮しました。

1)「聞く」「読む」「話す」に「書く」活動を加え、4技能のバランスがとれた学習活動を実現。

2) 患者が初めて来院する場面や問診票の記入を依頼する場面を追加。

3) 海外の看護事情に目を開き、幅広い視野を持てるように読み物をリニューアル。

4) 医療現場で使用頻度の高い症状名と病名を再選考。

その読み物の中で、看護師を目指すみなさんに力強いメッセージをくださいました故日野原重明氏、「国境なき医師団」に参加した経験を書いてくださった小林さくら氏にこの場を借りてお礼を申し上げます。また、医療現場で必要な英語表現のアンケートに答えてくださった多くの看護師さん、興味のある話題についてのアンケートに答えてくれた多くの看護学生に深く感謝いたします。

本書の出版にあたっては、私たちが人生のさまざまな場所で出会った多くの方々に後押しをしていただきました。西谷千恵氏（元中京学院大学看護学部）からは看護の専門家としての協力を、井手初穂氏（愛知国際病院）、今井常夫氏（国立病院機構東名古屋病院長）、押味貴之氏（国際医療福祉大学医学部）からは医師としての専門知識や助言を、笹川いづみ氏（東京白十字病院）と佐藤まりこ氏からは看護師としての意見を、神谷昌明氏（豊田工業高等専門学校）からはコーパス の助言を、Karen Fenwick 氏と James Venema 氏、Alexandra Burke 氏、Patrice Pendell 氏には英語の校正を、また、ナショナルジオグラフィック ラーニングの吉田剛氏、編集者の水越由美子氏には魅力ある教科書にするための協力や助言をしていただきました。写真の撮影では名古屋市立大学病院、初台あらいクリニックにご協力いただきました。皆様に心から感謝いたします。

井上真紀・佐藤利哉

Scope and Sequence

Unit	Titles	Dialog	Vocabulary Building	Let's Listen
	Target skill	Communicating	Vocabulary	Listening skill (key words
1	**Power of Language**			
2	**Don't worry.**	Giving encouragement	Hospital departments	injury / rash / burn / stomach pain
3	**How may I help you?**	Helping with registration at hospital	Body parts	full name / language / hospital ID card / emergency
4	**How are you feeling?**	Asking about feelings	Internal organs	ulcer/ delivery / leg pain / coughing
5	**Could you fill in this medical questionnaire?**	Filling in medical questionnaires	Diseases (internal medicine)	myoma / breaking a bone / Caesarean section / neck brace
6	**Take the elevator, please.**	Giving directions in hospitals	Diseases and injuries	toothache / urine test / diaper / pharmacy
7	**What are your symptoms?**	Asking about symptoms	Symptoms in the upper body	headache / chest pain / sore throat / painful urination
8	**Where does it hurt?**	Asking about pain	Symptoms in the lower body	joint pain / back pain / sprain / swollen eyelid
9	**How long have you had these symptoms?**	Asking about the duration of symptoms	General symptoms	itch / wheeze / tiredness / palpitation, shortness of breath
10	**I'm going to take a blood sample.**	Explaining tests and treatments	Tests and examinations	IV drip / injection / urine test / X-ray
11	**Let me take your vital signs.**	Taking vital signs	Medical terms 1	meal time / bath time / medicine time / bedsore
12	**Your surgery will be tomorrow.**	Explaining the pre-surgery protocol	Anesthesia and pain	meals / sleeping pills / anesthesia / painkiller
13	**There are three kinds of medicine.**	Explaining about medicines	Kinds of medicine	tablet / ointment / capsule / suppository
14	**Are you worried about anything?**	Asking about worries of the patient	Medical terms 2	Muslim / delivery / Hindu / Kampo medicine
15	**It's time to be discharged.**	Giving advice about life after discharge	Abbreviations	working / salt intake / exercise / outpatient visit

	Let's Read	Let's Write
Speaking skill	Reading skill	Writing skill
	Power of Language A message from Dr. Hinohara	
Giving encouragement	Technical terms used at hospitals	
The opening conversation	'*Namaste*: I Am Mother Teresa'	Writing reasons
Asking about feelings	Talking about your pain.	Writing opinions
Asking about medical history	Touchy-Feely Stuff	Describing ideal nurses
Asking and answering questions about directions	A Nurse on Mars? Why Not?	Writing opinions
Asking about symptoms	Nurses Know	Writing about one's own experience
Asking about pain	Awakenings	Writing about the joy of life
Asking about the duration of symptoms	Animal-Assisted Therapy: Domestic animals aren't merely pets. To some, they can be healers.	Writing opinions
Explaining how tests and treatments are given	Surviving the Night Shift: Making *Zeitgeber* work for you.	Writing opinions
Explaining how care is given at hospital	A Smart Doctor Listens to the Nurses	Writing about a hospital department
Explaining pre- or post-surgery treatment	Sexual Harassment in the Workplace	Writing opinions
Explaining how to take different kinds of medicine	The Art of Saying Yes	Writing about professional skills
Asking patients if something is worrying them	'To the Nurse Who Knows My Name . . .'	Writing opinions
Giving advice on what to do when they leave hospital	Overseas Volunteer	Writing opinions

本書の構成と効果的な使い方

本書は、初めて医療英語を学ぶ学生や、基礎的な医療英語の力をつけたいと考えている人たちが、楽しみながら、英語の4技能（聞く、読む、話す、書く力）をバランスよく身につけられるように構成されています。

まず、Unit 1 では、言葉そのものとどのように向き合うべきなのか、また医療従事者がなぜ英語を身につける必要があるのかを学んでください。次に、Unit 2 ～ 15 は、約900人の現役の看護師が答えたアンケート調査に基づき、臨床現場のさまざまな場面で必要な英語表現の聞き取りや会話練習、医療専門用語の学習、また、医療に関する英語記事を読む学習から、自分の思いを英語で表現する学習まで、医療英語を飽きることなく幅広く学べるように工夫しました。

ユニットの基本構成

Dialog

「医療現場でどのような英語表現が必要ですか」という問いへの回答に基づき、必要性の高い英語表現を優先して盛り込んであります。どの表現も、外国人患者のケアをするときには、すぐに使えるものばかりです。音声を注意深く聞き、看護師役と患者役のペアになって読む練習をし、時間をかけて会話を丸ごと覚えてしまいましょう。ひとつの文章を一気に覚えられないときは、意味の切れ目で切って部分ごとに覚えて最後につないでみましょう。英語を使って、にこやかに外国人患者とコミュニケーションをとっている自分を思い描きましょう。

Vocabulary Building

コーパス（英語の膨大なデータベース）の情報を使って、医療分野で使用頻度の高い語を選び、厚生労働省の統計や臨床現場の看護師と医師の意見を参考に、看護に関する専門用語を厳選してあります。それらの専門用語は、外国人患者とコミュニケーションをとるとき、カルテに出てくる用語を理解するとき、医療分野の文献を読み取るときなど、知っていると役に立つものばかりです。

医療現場では、外国人患者とのコミュニケーションに必要とされる、病気や症状に関する一般的な語彙や表現と、カルテや文献に出てくる略語や専門用語とが混在しています。それらの用語を Unit ごとに少しずつ広く学べるようにしてあります。問題を解いた後で、何度も音読して、自力で読めるようにしましょう。

まず、これらの医療英単語の意味を理解し、その後、それらを日本語から英語に変換できるかどうか試してみましょう。医療英語を使いこなせるようになるには、英語から日本語へと理解するだけでなく、余裕があったら日本語から英語へと訳して発話する練習をしましょう。

Let's Listen

A 看護師と患者の会話を聞いて、要点をつかみましょう。最初からすべての単語を完璧に聞き取ろうとするより、key words に焦点をあてて意味を推測することにより、患者が訴えている症状や、患者が尋ねていることなどを聞き取るようにしましょう。

B 2回目に聞くときは、質問に答えたり、指示を与えたり、説明をしたりする看護師の言葉にも注意してみましょう。枠の中の英語表現は次の練習問題で発話する言葉ですから、聞き取りが終わったら暗記するほど何度も読みましょう。

C 聞き取りをした会話の中で、看護師に必要な英語表現が日本語になっています。看護師役と患者役のペアになって、役割交代をしながら、すらすらと読んだり訳したりできるようになるまで練習しましょう。看護師の言葉がうまく言えないときは、前のページを確認しても構いませんが、数回読んで覚えてから、ペア・ワークに戻りましょう。

Let's Read

英文を読むことを通して、看護の世界における視野が広がるように、それぞれの Unit に幅広い話題の読み物を選びました。多くは *American Journal of Nursing* というアメリカの看護雑誌から抜粋し、読みやすく編集してあります。このほかに看護の業界用語、看護学生にぜひ見てほしい映画の紹介、専門家から看護学生へのメッセージなど、バラエティーに富んだ内容を楽しんでください。

それぞれの読み物は、一語ずつ訳すより、まずは練習問題を解くことによって概要を理解するようにしてください。医療用語や使用頻度の低い語句は右側の注を参考にしながら読んでください。時間が許せば、音読にも挑戦してみましょう。

Let's Write

Unit の最後で、それまでに読んだ内容について感じたことや考えたことを少し英語で表現してみましょう。

英語を学ぶときは、聞いたり読んだりして INPUT したことを参考に、話したり書いたりして OUTPUT する、というサイクルを意識するとより効果的に学習することができます。そうすることが「学んだ英語表現を実際に使えるようになる」近道なのです。

UNIT 1 Power of Language

言葉の力について

私たちが当たり前のように毎日使っている「言葉」―その一つ一つの言葉は、それを使う人間全体の世界を背負っています。それは日本語でも英語でも同じです。英語を使うときも、やはり言葉はそれを使う人の世界を背負うことになります。たとえ英語が不完全であっても、またそれをどんな場で使うことになっても、あなたの口から出た言葉は、あなたがどんな人なのかを相手に伝えることになります。プロの看護師として心のこもったケアをするならば、それは、あなたが使う英語を通して外国人患者にもちゃんと伝わるはずです。

Passage 1

Power of Language

A-02

（原著「言葉の力」大岡信）

People often discuss what they consider to be "beautiful words" and "correct words." However, words do not exist on their own. A beautiful word spoken by someone may not sound as beautiful when spoken by someone else. This is because words are not just literal tools, but inevitably carry the whole background of the speaker. The whole being of a speaker is reflected in each tiny word, so to speak.

When I was talking with Fukumi Shimura, a kimono dyer who lives in Kyoto, she showed me a kimono woven from thread that brought to mind the incredibly beautiful color of cherry blossoms. The pink color was pale but held a flaming strength inside, brilliant and calm at the same time. I felt my eyes and heart being pulled into its beauty.

"How did you extract this color?" I asked.

"From cherry trees," she answered.

I naively imagined that she extracted the color by boiling down the petals of cherry blossoms, but actually it was the bark of cherry trees that was used. She extracted this beautiful pink color from the rough black bark.

She continued to explain that you can't get this exceptionally beautiful color at just any season of the year. Just before the blossom season, and using the bark of cherry trees growing in mountains, you can produce the indescribably beautiful blushing color, she said.

When I heard this story, I was shaken by a mysterious feeling. In early spring, just before it is to blossom, a cherry tree mobilizes every part of its being, not just the petals alone, to produce the most incredible shade of pink. The pink showing on the petals is the pink that is sent forth from the trunk, the bark and the sap. All parts of the tree get tinted pink in spring, and the pink petals are just a small part of it.

I feel the same can be said about language. Each word corresponds to each petal of a cherry blossom. Though its color is nothing like that of the soft pink petals, the thick trunk is what really produces the intense pink that bursts forth from the cherry blossoms. We should think of language in the same way. Only then will we come close to understanding what is meant by "beautiful words" and "correct words."

Vocabulary

4 **literal** 文字通りの
5 **inevitably** 必然的に
7 **dyer** 染色家
8 **weave** …を織る（woven = 過去分詞）
9 **cherry blossom** 桜の花
pale 淡い
10 **flaming** 燃えるような
brilliant 色鮮やかな
12 **extract** …を絞り取る
14 **naively** 短絡的に
15 **petal** 花びら
bark 木の皮
18 **exceptionally** 並外れて
21 **indescribably** 言いようのないほどに
blushing 赤みがかった
23 **mobilize** …を結集する
24 **shade** 色合い
26 **trunk** 幹
sap 樹液
tint …に色合いを付ける
28 **correspond to** …に相当する
30 **intense** 鮮やかな

Q 筆者は、桜の花びら１枚と言葉の１語とにどのような共通点を見出したのでしょうか。

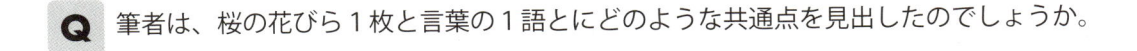

日野原重明先生は、105 歳で亡くなるまで医師として患者の診察を続け、日本人が健やかに生きることができるように、医療従事者にだけでなく子供や高齢者にも向けて、幅広く提言し続けました。日野原先生から看護師を目指すみなさんへのメッセージです。

Passage 2

A message from Dr. Hinohara

A-03

Today, nurses are expected to have an international education and be able to communicate well in English. With such preparation, nurses will be able to play significant roles when, for example, they work in English-speaking regions as volunteers.

I hope you, for whom this textbook was written, will learn to understand spoken English, and be able to speak in simple but polite English. This is because you are expected to become professionals who can provide adequate care while using the English language.

So let me give you a piece of advice: you should always remember, when you learn basic English conversation, that you are learning this to develop yourself as a professional nurse.

The most important thing you should keep in mind is that you are training to become a nurse who has a compassionate character as well as professional skills.

Here I would like to introduce a passage from the commencement address to the Johns Hopkins nurses on May 7, 1913, given by Professor William Osler (1849-1919).

"There are seven virtues for a nurse: tact, tidiness,
taciturnity, sympathy, gentleness, cheerfulness,
all linked together by charity."

"Aequanimitas—With Other Addresses to Medical Students, Nurses and Practitioners of Medicine" (McGraw-Hill, 1906) by Sir William

Osler is also recommended reading for you. You will learn a great deal on humanity and medicine from this book. His words will be very helpful when you care for English-speaking patients.

I hope you will learn to communicate from your heart when you are a nurse, that is to say, to "give an infusion" of your precious time to your patients. Do put your heart into learning, learn to become a clear and polite speaker of English, and always speak with a warm smile.

Honorary Director, St. Luke's International Hospital, Tokyo
Honorary President, St. Luke's International University
Shigeaki Hinohara

Vocabulary

13 **compassionate** 思いやりのある
15- **commencement address** 卒業式の式辞
16 **Johns Hopkins** ジョンズ・ホプキンズ大学
18 **virtue** 徳
tact 機転
tidiness 几帳面さ
19 **taciturnity** 寡黙
cheerfulness 快活さ
20 **charity** 慈愛の心
21 **Aequanimitas** （ラテン語）平静の心
22 **practitioner of medicine** 医師
24 **humanity** 人間性
27 **infusion** 点滴

Q 空欄を埋めて、日野原先生からのアドバイスの内容を完成させましょう。

基礎的な英会話を学ぶときに覚えておくべきことは、__________

____

心に留めておくべき最も重要なことは、__________

____

UNIT 2 Don't worry.

励ましの声をかけましょう

A nurse helping a patient at reception

一人で外国に住んでいることを想像してみてください。まだ友達は少なく、家族は近くにいません。その国の言葉にも習慣にもまだ慣れていません。そんなときに病気にかかったとしたら、どんなに不安で心細いことでしょう。恐る恐る行った病院で優しい言葉を一言でもかけてもらったら、どんなにうれしく、心強く感じることでしょうか。

Dialog

A-04

Nurse

How may I help you?

My daughter has a high fever. Her temperature was 40 degrees at home. I want her to see a doctor as soon as possible.

Please calm down. Could you speak more slowly?

My daughter has a high fever. Her temperature was 40 degrees at home. I want her to see a doctor as soon as possible.

Patient's mother

OK. Please go to Pediatrics. Don't worry. She'll be fine. The doctor will see your daughter soon.

Vocabulary

fever /fíːvər/ 熱　**temperature** /témp(ə)rətʃər/ 体温　**Pediatrics** /pìːdiǽtrɪks/ 小児科

A-05

Variations

- 大丈夫ですよ。　It's all right now.　It'll be all right.　You'll be OK.
- 落ち着いて。　Relax.　Please stay calm.
- 良い調子です。　You're doing well.
- 早く良くなるといいですね。　I hope you'll feel better soon.
- わかります。　I understand.

Vocabulary Building

A-06

1～13の用語の意味を調べて空欄に書きましょう。また、イラストのa～mの患者が行くべきところを選び、番号で答えましょう。

a. ☐

b. ☐
c. ☐
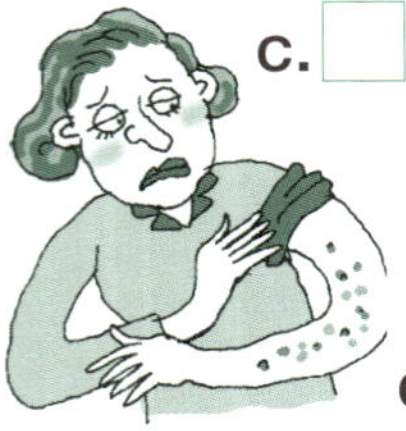

d. ☐
e. ☐

1. Internal Medicine /ɪntə̀ːrn(ə)l méds(ə)n/ [ ]
2. Ophthalmology /ɑ̀(ː)fθælmɑ́(ː)lədʒi/ [ ]
3. Obstetrics / Gynecology [/]
   /əbstétrɪks/ /gàɪnɪkɑ́(ː)lədʒi, dʒàɪ-/
   OB-GYN /aubiːgáɪn, -dʒín/ [ ]
4. ENT /ìːentíː/ (Ear, Nose and Throat) [ ]
5. Dermatology /də̀ːrmətɑ́(ː)lədʒi/ [ ]
6. Psychiatry /saɪkɑ́(ɪ)ətri/ [ ]
7. Pediatrics /pìːdiǽtrɪks/ [ ]
8. Surgery /sə́ːrdʒ(ə)ri/ [ ]
9. Dentistry /déntəstri/ [ ]
10. Urology /ju(ə)rɑ́(ː)lədʒi/ [ ]
11. Radiology /rèɪdiɑ́(ː)lədʒi/ [ ]
12. Orthopedics /ɔ̀ːrθəpíːdɪks/ [ ]
13. ER / Emergency Room /ɪmə́ːrdʒ(ə)nsi ruːm/ [ ]

f. ☐

g. ☐
h. ☐

i. ☐

j. ☐
k. ☐

l. ☐
m. ☐

Hints

dent- (tooth)	dermato- (skin)	gyneco- (woman)	ophthalmo- (eye)	
ortho- (correct)	ped- (child)	psych- (mind)	radio- (radiation)	uro- (urine)

Let's Listen

A-07 ▶ 10

A 4人の患者やその家族と看護師の会話を聞き、患者の症状についての key words を英語で書き取りましょう。また、その内容を key words から推測して日本語で書いてみましょう。

	key words	症状
1		
2		
3		
4		

B 同じ会話をもう1度聞きましょう。それぞれの患者にかける励ましの言葉を枠内から選び、記号で答えましょう。そして意味を考えながら、暗記するまで何度も読んでみましょう。

1 ____　2 ____　3 ____　4 ____

a. I hope you'll be better soon.
b. Please try not to worry so much.
c. Don't worry. It'll be all right.
d. I understand. Please calm down.

Vocabulary

injure /ín(d)ʒər/ …をけがする　**blood** /blʌd/ 血　**worried** /wə́ːrid/ 心配して
Neurosurgery /njùərousə́ːrdʒəri/ 脳神経外科　**rash** /ræʃ/ 発疹
nursery school /nə́ːrs(ə)ri skùːl/ 保育園　**chicken pox** /tʃíkɪn pɑ̀(ː)ks/ 水疱瘡
burn /bəːrn/ …をやけどする　**pain** /peɪn/ 痛み　**stomach** /stʌ́mək/ 胃
throw up /θròʊ ʌ́p/ 吐く　**cancer** /kǽnsər/ がん

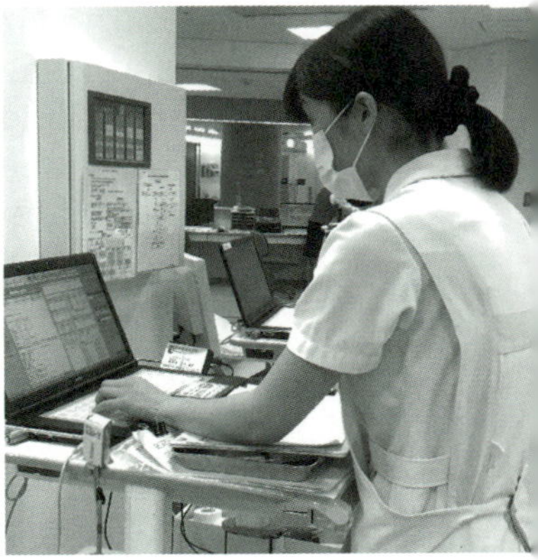

C ペアになって、患者と看護師のセリフを声に出して言ってみましょう。看護師役は前のページを参考にして、英語の言い回しを考えてみましょう。

1

My son has injured his head. He fell and hit his head on the corner of the desk. There was a lot of blood! I'm really worried.

わかりました。
落ち着いてください。
We'll send you to Neurosurgery.

2

I found a small rash on my daughter's face last night. Today, she has a rash all over her body. I heard some kids at her nursery school have chicken pox.

心配しないでください。
良くなりますよ。
Please go to Pediatrics.

3

I have burned my left hand. Yesterday, I was frying chicken for dinner. Suddenly, the oil burst into flames. I tried to put out the fire and burned my hand.

早く良くなるといいですね。
Let me take you to Dermatology.

4

I've been having a lot of stomach pain recently. I can't eat and throw up sometimes. I'm afraid I have stomach cancer. I'm so worried.
あまり心配しないようにしてください。
I'll show you to Internal Medicine.

Let's Learn Useful Knowledge

看護師の世界では英語やドイツ語などの外国語に由来する「業界用語」があります。そのため、日本人同士の会話でも外国語が使われることがあります。語源と意味を知っておきましょう。

A ナース・ステーションでの看護師 A さんと後輩の B さんの会話です。あなたは理解できますか。会話で使われた用語の意味を辞書で調べて次の表に記入しましょう。

A: 201 号室の佐藤さんの ❶**バイタル**とった？

B: はい、30 分前にとりました。術後は良好です。あとは ❷**メタ**がないといいですけど…。

A: 点滴の管理はくれぐれも慎重にね。漏れて ❸**ネクロ**ったらたいへんだから。

B: はい。昨日の ❹**ディーエム**の患者さん、❺**アンプタ**しなくても大丈夫ですって。先生がそう言っていました。

A: 205 号室の井上さん？　それはよかったわ。でも井上さん、また ❻**タキ**ってくるかもしれないから気をつけていて。

B: わかりました。❼**心カテ**の検査が入りましたので、今から行ってきます。

A-11

❶	バイタル	vital	/váɪt(ə)l/	
❷	メタ	metastasis	/metǽstəsɪs/	
❸	ネクロ	necrosis	/nekróusɪs/	
❹	ディーエム	diabetes mellitus	/dà(ɪ)əbíːtiːz məláɪtəs/	
❺	アンプタ	amputation	/æ̀mpjətéɪʃ(ə)n/	
❻	タキ	tachycardia	/tæ̀kəkáːrdiə/	
❼	心カテ	cardiac catheter	/káːrdiæ̀k kǽθətər/	

B 次の用語の意味は何でしょう？　答えは右下の語群にあります。例にならって記号を選び、その意味を日本語に直して（　　）に入れましょう。

1　例）

急患よ。すぐに
オペ（　　d. 手術　　）
の用意をして。

アッペ（　　　　　　）
だって？
受け入れ準備 OK だよ。

2

悪いんだけど
ギネ（　　　　　　）
に行ってくれる？

いいよ。このカルテを
ウロ（　　　　　　）
に届けてからね。

3

4

- **a.** suction /sʌ́kʃ(ə)n/
- **b.** Urology /ju(ə)rɑ́(:)lədʒi/
- **c.** asthma /ǽzmə/
- **d.** operation /ɑ̀pəréɪʃ(ə)n/
- **e.** Gynecology /gàɪnɪkɑ́(:)lədʒi, dʒàɪ-/
- **f.** appendicitis /əpèndəsáɪtəs/
- **g.** cooling /kú:lɪŋ/
- **h.** dementia /dɪménʃə/

業界用語は、一部を除き、学習研究社刊「ナースのための病院で使う英会話」（飯田恭子監修）より引用・改作しました。

ドイツ語由来の用例

「アナムネをとる」	既往歴（Anamnese）を聞き取る
「ワイセが高い」	白血球（Weiße Blutkörperchen）の数値が高い
「ステる」	死亡する（sterben）

UNIT 3 How may I help you?

どうなさいましたか

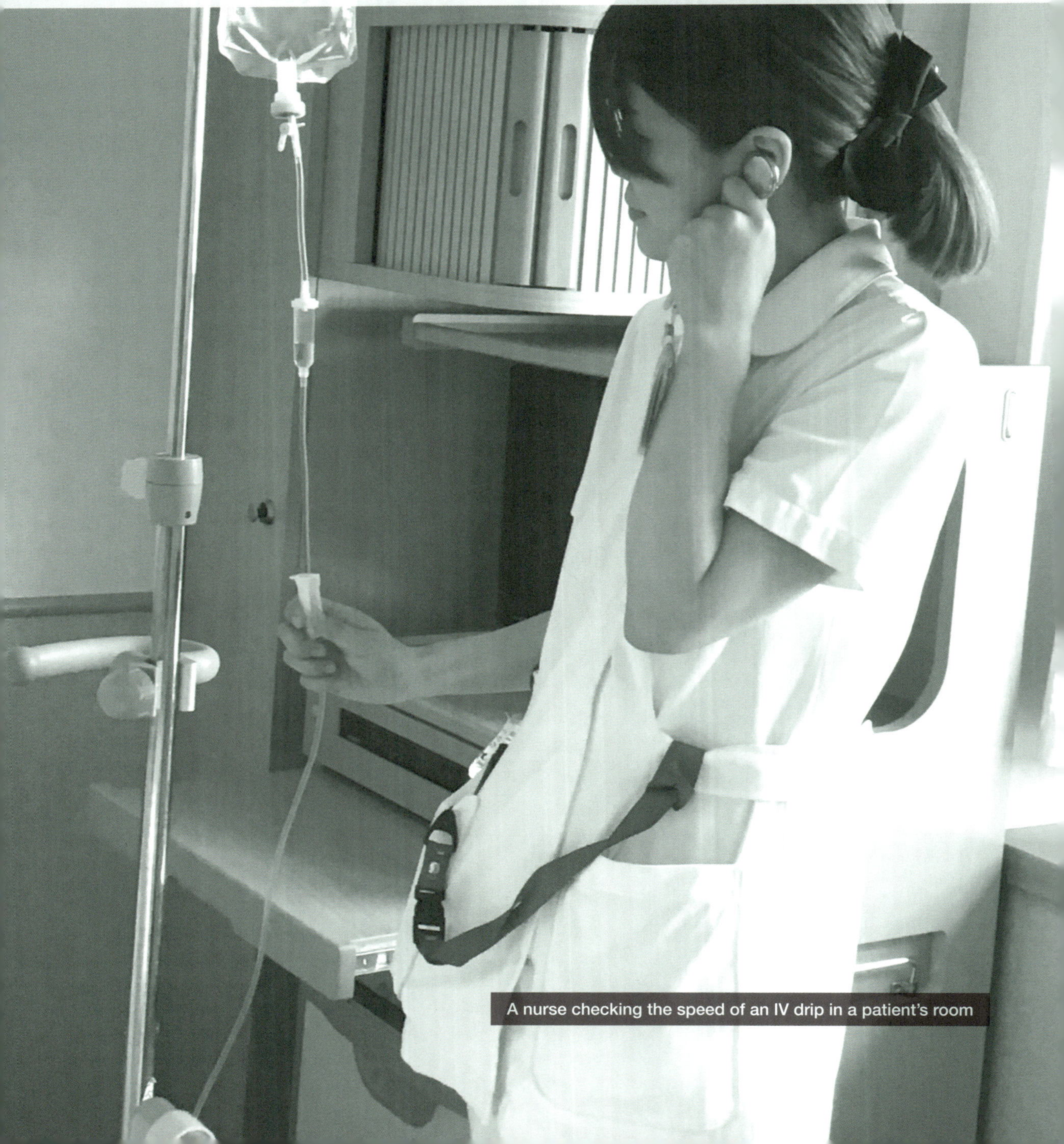

A nurse checking the speed of an IV drip in a patient's room

病院で困った様子の外国人患者を見かけたら、勇気を出して声をかけ、初診の手続きを進めてあげましょう。そのときに、"May I ～" や "Could you ～" などの丁寧な英語表現を使うと、言葉のメッセージだけでなく、「私はあなたに丁寧に接したい」という温かい心のメッセージも同時に伝わります。

Dialog

A-12

Nurse

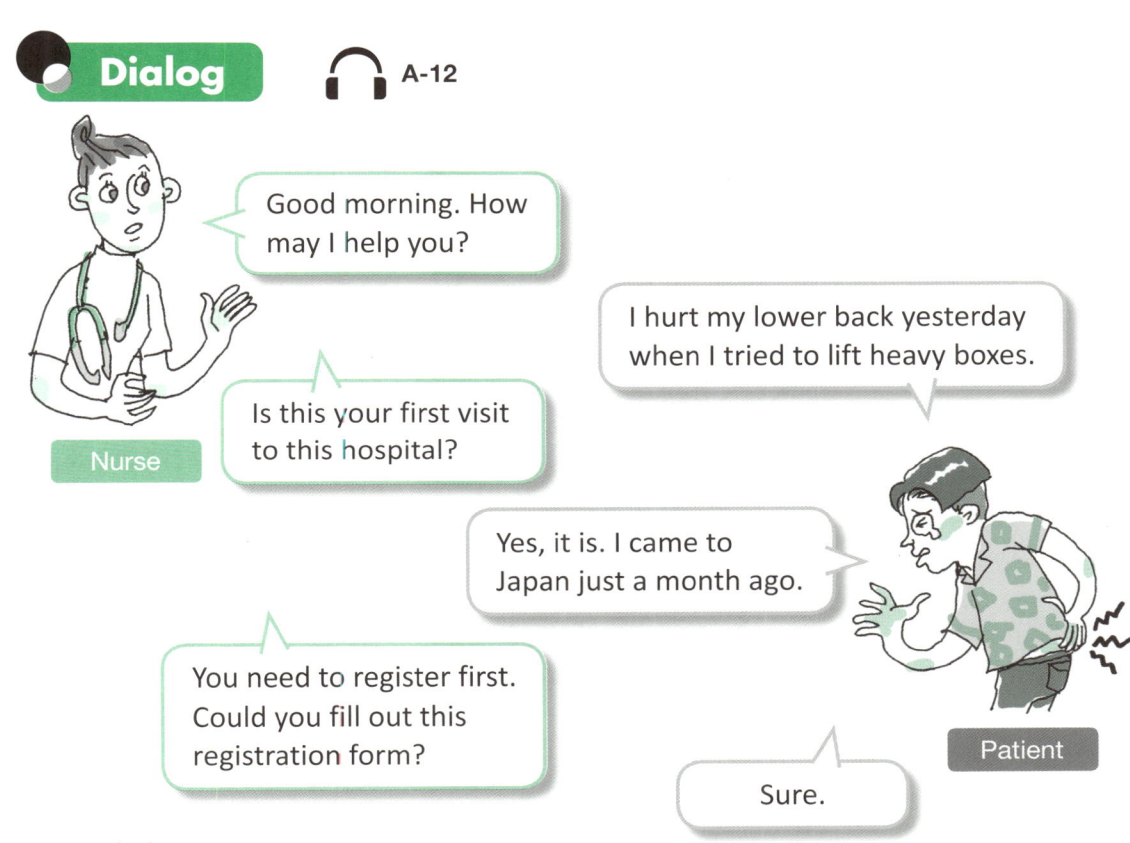

Nurse: Good morning. How may I help you?

Patient: I hurt my lower back yesterday when I tried to lift heavy boxes.

Nurse: Is this your first visit to this hospital?

Patient: Yes, it is. I came to Japan just a month ago.

Nurse: You need to register first. Could you fill out this registration form?

Patient: Sure.

Patient

Vocabulary

insurance /ɪnʃʊ́ər(ə)ns/ 保険　**referral letter** /rifə́r(ə)l létər/ 紹介状

A-13

Variations

- どうなさいましたか。　**May I help you? / What can I do for you?**
- 健康保険に加入していますか。　**Do you have any health insurance?**
- 紹介状をお持ちですか。　**Do you have a referral letter?**

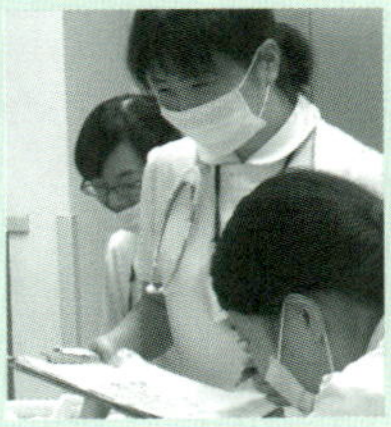

Vocabulary Building

A-14

体の名称を表す語句を枠内から選び、正しい位置に書き入れましょう。

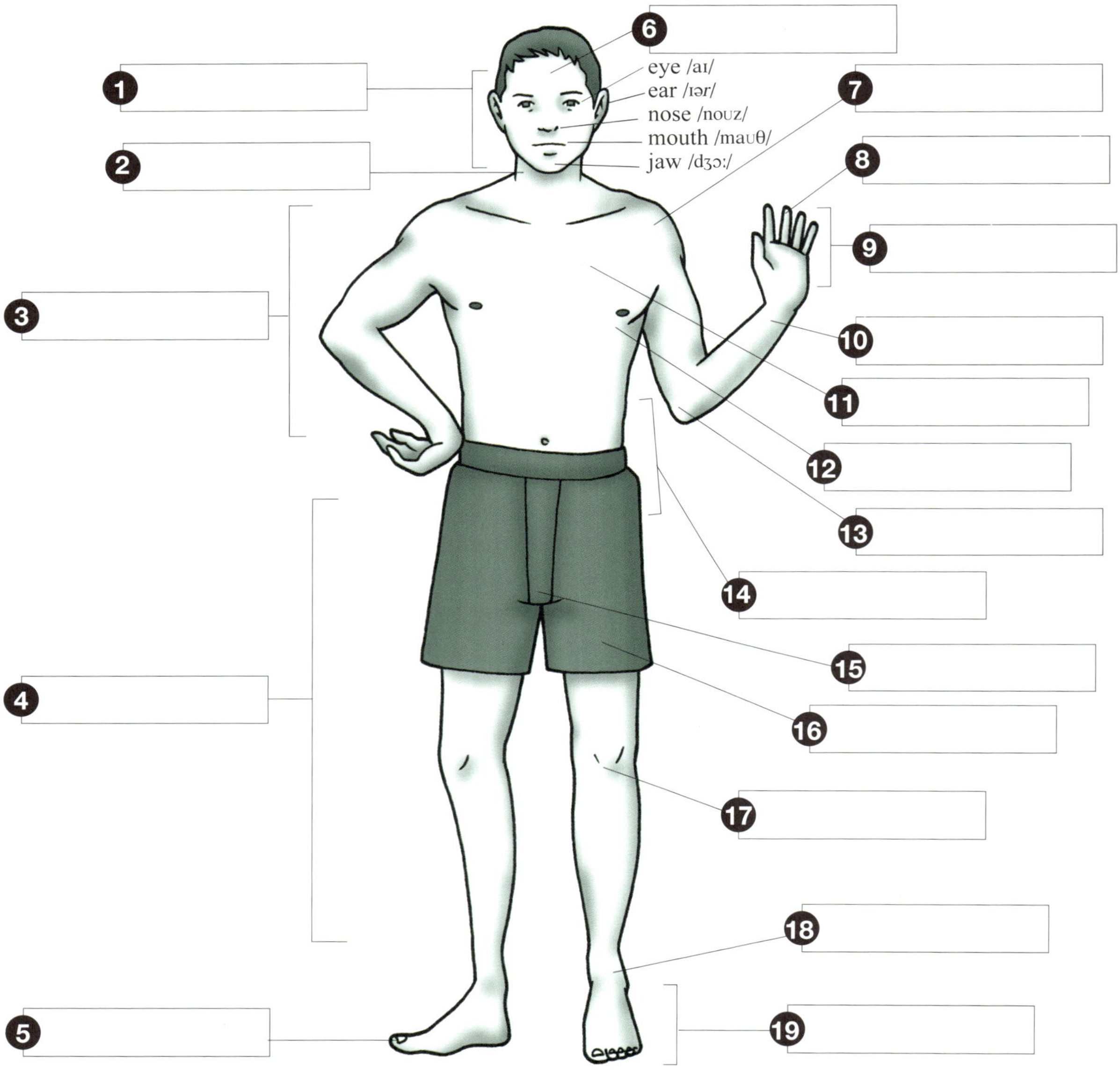

abdomen /ǽbdəmən, æbdóʊ-/	**ankle** /ǽŋk(ə)l/	**arm** /ɑːrm/	**breast** /brest/
chest /tʃest/	**elbow** /élboʊ/	**face** /feɪs/	**finger** /fíŋgər/
foot /fʊt/	**forehead** /fɔ́ːrhèd/	**hand** /hænd/	**knee** /niː/
leg /leg/	**neck** /nek/	**private parts** /práɪvət pɑ̀ːrts/	
shoulder /ʃóʊldər/	**thigh** /θaɪ/	**toe** /toʊ/	**wrist** /rɪst/

Let's Listen

A-15 ▶ 18

A 4 人の患者と看護師の会話を聞き、患者の返答についての key words を英語で書き取りましょう。また、その内容を key words から推測して日本語で書いてみましょう。

	key words	患者の返答
1		
2		
3		
4		

B 同じ会話をもう 1 度聞きましょう。それぞれの患者への適切な指示や質問を枠内から選び、記号で答えましょう。そして意味を考えながら、暗記するまで何度も読んでみましょう。

1 ____ 2 ____ 3 ____ 4 ____

a. I see. Let me ask you some questions to prepare for the hospital ID card.
b. I see. May I have your full name, please?
c. Who may I contact in case of any emergency?
d. Do you speak any other languages other than your native language?

Vocabulary

lightheaded /laɪthédɪd/ 頭がふらふらする **appetite** /ǽpɪtàɪt/ 食欲
Portuguese /pɔ̀ːtʃugíːz/ ポルトガル語 **Turkey** /tə́ːrki/ トルコ
hospital ID card /há(ː)spɪt(ə)l àɪdíː kɑːrd/ 診察券

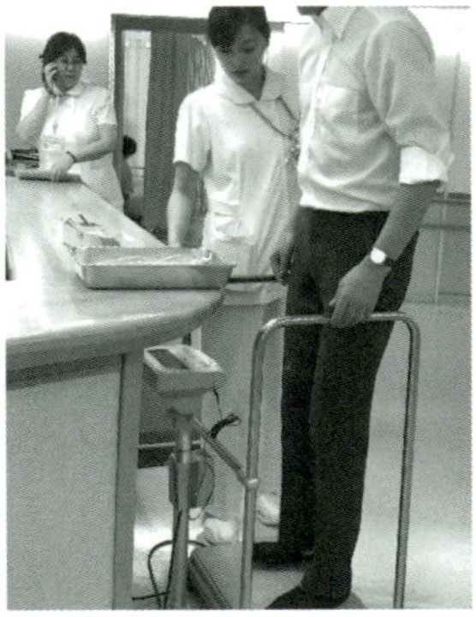

C ペアになって、患者と看護師のセリフを声に出して言ってみましょう。看護師役は前のページを参考にして、英語の言い回しを考えてみましょう。

1

Nurse
Good morning. どうなさいましたか。

Patient
I feel sick and lightheaded in the morning these days. Also I have no appetite.

Nurse
わかりました。フルネームをいただけますか。

2

N Hello. どうなさいましたか。

P I have a very bad headache. I can't speak Japanese. I'm from Brazil. I speak Portuguese.

N 母語以外の言語は話しますか。

3

N この病院には初めてですか。

P Yes, I came to Japan two months ago. I've come from Turkey.

N わかりました。診察券を用意するためにいくつか質問をしますね。

4

N この病院には初めてですか。

P Yes. As this is my first time to get sick in Japan, I'm worried and feel scared.

N 緊急の場合は、どなたに連絡をとればよいですか。

Let's Read

A-19

次の文章は、看護師である筆者がマザー・テレサと出会ったときの、忘れられない貴重な体験を書いたものです。筆者は 14 歳のとき、感染症の専門医である父親と一緒にカルカッタを訪れました。そこで、貧困と不幸のどん底にいるハンセン病患者の治療にあたっていたマザー・テレサと出会いました。マザー・テレサは小柄で、目は明るくくっきりとして、口元は優しく、強い意志を秘めていました。

'*Namaste*: I Am Mother Teresa'

IT IS YOUR TURN TO GIVE

Next morning in the camp there were about 50 people with various stages of leprosy: wounds oozing pus, hands and legs amputated, ears and noses half-eaten by disease. My heart pounded. I just wanted to go back home. Then Mother Teresa told me, "Now it is your turn to give something to others." She tugged on my hand. I was no longer afraid. Following the nuns' example, I started gently cleaning wounds with cotton cloths soaked in an antiseptic solution.

A boy whose face had been mostly eaten away by leprosy was sitting in the corner of the room. He had no hair and both legs had been amputated. His eyes, however, were big, brown, and beautiful.

I began to pat his shoulder. He looked up, surprised, unaccustomed to touch. His name was Gopal. He was alone. His father had died of leprosy when Gopal was a baby, and his mother died a week ago. Tears flowed down his cheeks. He was 14. I, too, was 14, but he looked like a 7-year-old. "I feel lonely here, everyone has their own friends. I do not want to die like my parents," Gopal said.

"You don't have to," I said. I explained how important food and medication are when fighting the disease. He slowly

Vocabulary

- title ***namaste*** ナマステ：ヒンドゥー教徒のあいさつ
- 3 **leprosy** ハンセン病
- **ooze** …をしみ出す
- **pus** 膿
- 4 **amputate** …を切断する
- 7 **tug** …を強く引く
- 8 **nun** 修道女
- 9 **soak** …を浸す
- **antiseptic** 殺菌された
- **solution** 溶液
- 15 **unaccustomed** 慣れていない
- 22 **medication** 薬

began to eat. Afterward, I cleaned his wounds with the antiseptic solution and gave him medication. As the days went by, I felt connected to this boy and spent most of my time with him. He gained weight and his face began to brighten. “What did you do to that boy?” the doctor asked. “I just gave him some attention and a little love,” I replied. I loved him as my little brother.

I WILL BE WAITING FOR YOU

On my last day at the camp, Gopal gave me a picture he had drawn of him and me. He said, “These have been the most wonderful days of my life. I want to grow up and help many people, like you do.” I hugged him and cried.

I wiped my tears, ran out, and found Mother Teresa. “I don’t want to go home. I want to become a nun, live here, and serve these people.” She smiled, placed her hand on my head, and said, “Go, child, become a nurse and come back. I will be waiting for you.” Still crying, I turned back to look at my little brother Gopal.

That was the last time I ever saw him.

Vocabulary

25 **connected** 気持ちが通じる

37 **serve** …に尽くす

A 出来事が起こった順に番号をつけましょう。

a ☐

b ☐

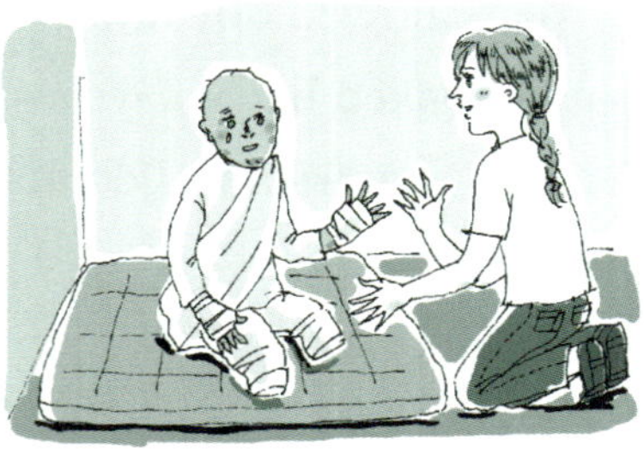

c ☐

d

e

f

B （　　）に入る適切な単語を枠内から選び、要約文を完成させましょう。

The writer, then a 14-year-old girl, went to Calcutta with her family. Her father was a doctor volunteering for WHO. She met Mother Teresa, who was serving people with ([1]　　　　). At first, she was not at ease in her new surroundings. But she was not ([2]　　　　) after Mother Teresa spoke to her. She started to take care of the patients. Then she met a boy, Gopal, who had a ([3]　　　　) case of leprosy. She became ([4]　　　　) with Gopal. Gopal was very ([5]　　　　) and appreciated his new friend. His face began to brighten when he saw her. On her last day, Gopal gave her a ([6]　　　　). The writer was sorry to say good-bye to Gopal. Mother Teresa told the writer to become a ([7]　　　　) and come back to India.

a. nurse	**b.** friends	**c.** picture	**d.** leprosy
e. lonely	**f.** afraid	**g.** serious	

Let's Write

質問に答えてみましょう。

Q. Why do you want to become a nurse?

A. ______________________________

____

UNIT 4 How are you feeling?

気分を聞いてみましょう

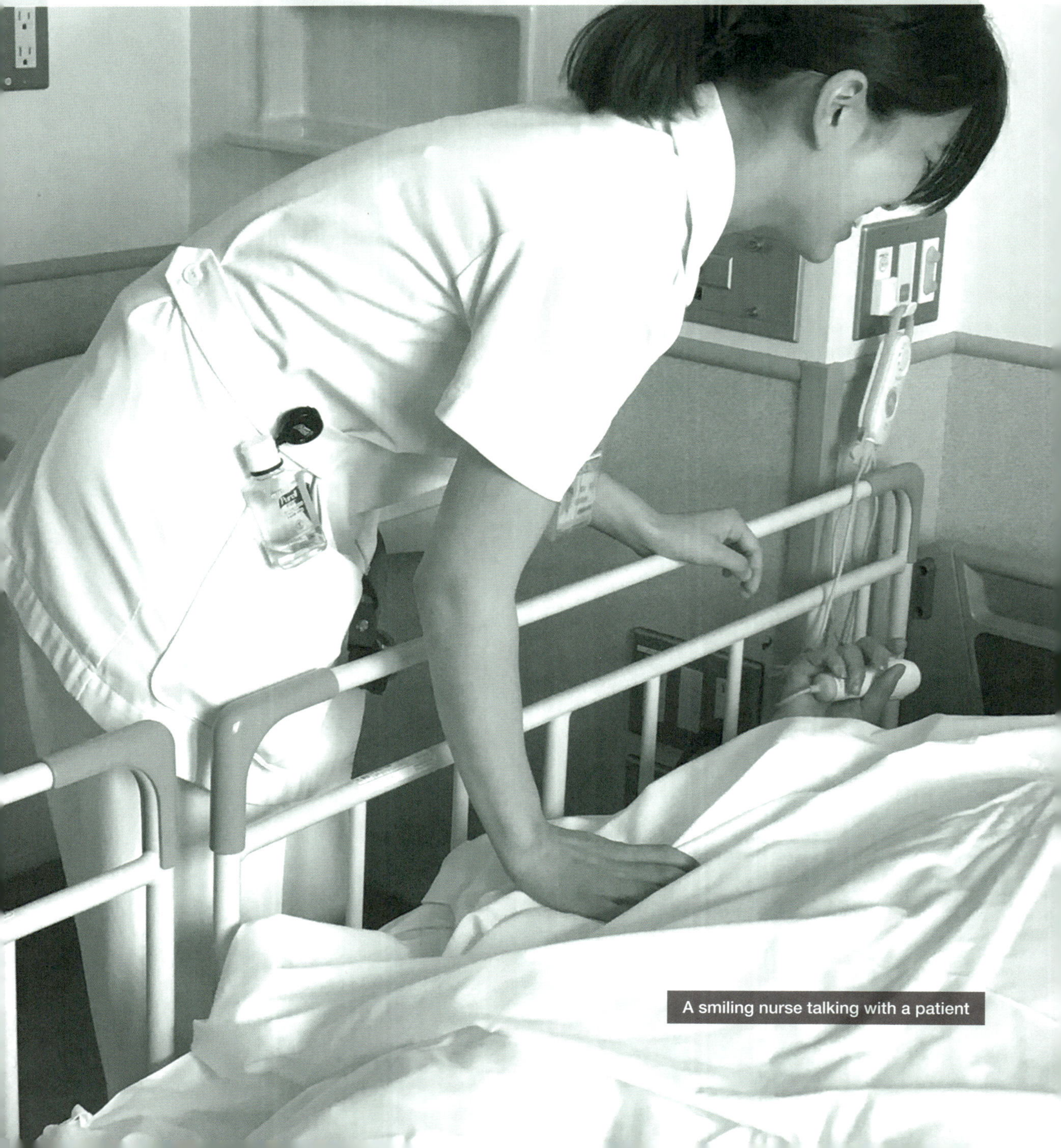

A smiling nurse talking with a patient

明るい笑顔で「おはようございます」とあいさつをされると、とても明るい気持ちになります。一方、しり込みしながら自信なさそうに小さな声であいさつされると不安になります。英語を使うときも同じです。明るくはっきりと、目を真っすぐに見てあいさつをすることが大切です。

Dialog

A-20

Nurse

Good morning. My name is Maki Inoue. I'm going to take care of you today.

Glad to meet you, Ms. Inoue. I'm John Ford. Thanks for seeing me.

Well, first of all, how are you feeling?

Not very well.

What seems to be the problem?

I feel a little dizzy.

Patient

Vocabulary

dizzy /dízi/ めまいがする

A-21

Variations

- 私はあなたの担当ナースです。 **I'm your nurse.** **I'll be your nurse.**
- ご気分はいかがですか。 **How do you feel?**
- あまり良くありません。 **Not very good.** **I don't feel very well.**
- 変わりありません。 **About the same.**
- 良いです。 **I'm fine.** **I feel all right.** **I feel good.**
- 少し／ずっと良くなりました。 **I feel a little / much better.**

Vocabulary Building

A-22

臓器の名称を表す語句を枠内から選び、正しい位置に書き入れましょう。

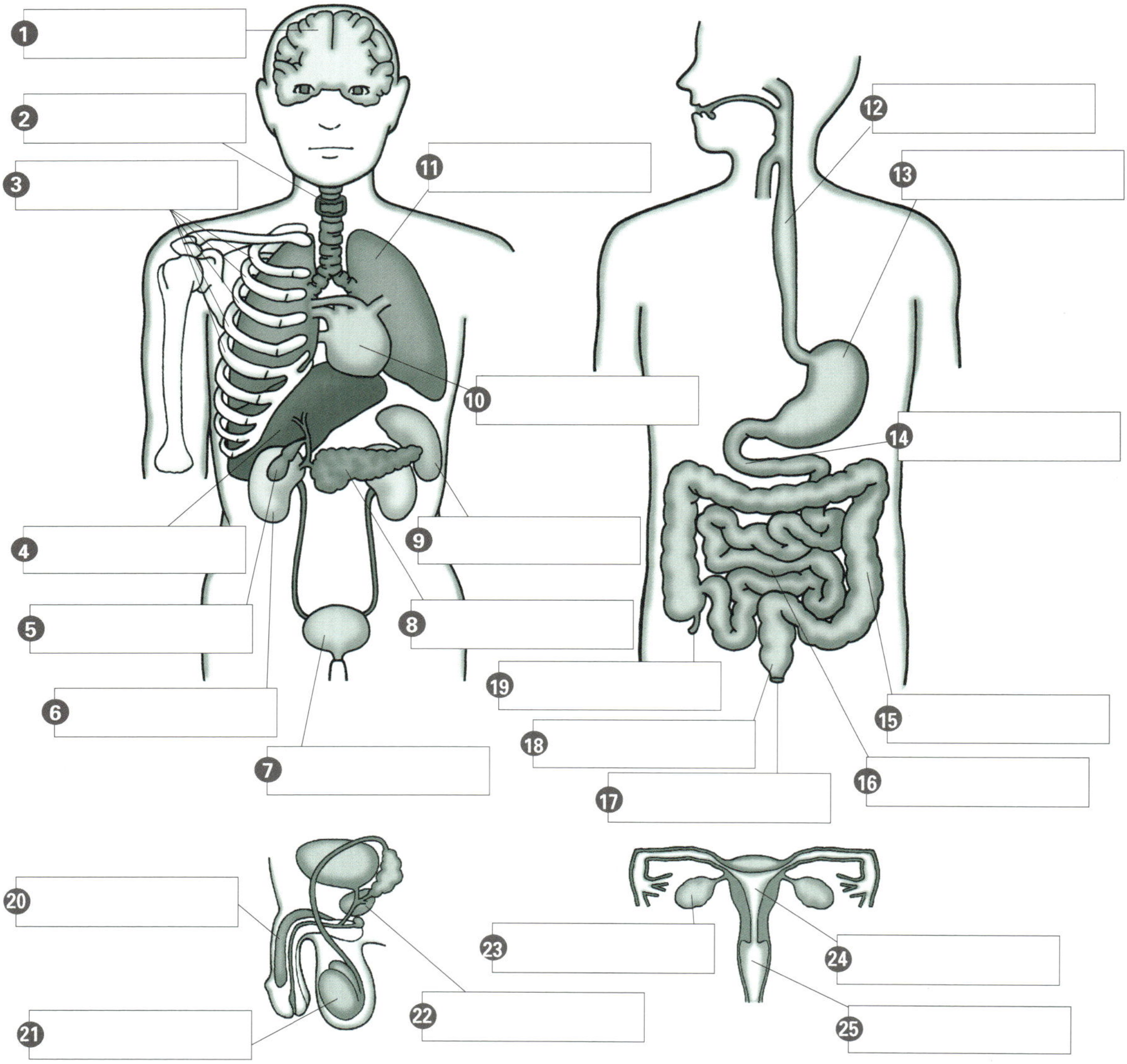

anus /éɪnəs/	**appendix** /əpéndɪks/	**bladder** /blǽdər/	**brain** /breɪn/
duodenum /djùːədíːnəm/	**esophagus** /ɪsáfəgəs/	**gall bladder** /gɔ́ːlblæ̀dər/	**heart** /hɑːrt/
kidney /kídni/	**large intestine** /lɑːrdʒ ɪntéstɪn/		**liver** /lívər/
lung /lʌŋ/	**ovary** /óʊv(ə)ri/	**pancreas** /pǽŋkriəs/	**penis** /píːnɪs/
prostate /prá(ː)steɪt/	**rectum** /réktəm/	**rib** /rɪb/	
small intestine /smɔːl ɪntéstɪn/		**spleen** /spliːn/	**stomach** /stʌ́mək/
testicle /téstɪk(ə)l/	**throat** /θroʊt/	**uterus** /júːt(ə)rəs/	**vagina** /vədʒáɪnə/

Let's Listen

A-23 ▶ 26

A 4人の患者と看護師の会話を聞き、患者の気分と症状についての key words を英語で書き取りましょう。また、その内容を key words から推測して日本語で書いてみましょう。

	key words	気分と症状
1		
2		
3		
4		

B 同じ会話をもう1度聞きましょう。それぞれの患者への適切な説明や指示を枠内から選び、記号で答えましょう。そして意味を考えながら、暗記するまで何度も読んでみましょう。

1 ____ 2 ____ 3 ____ 4 ____

a. Push the call button if you need anything.
b. Stomachache? The doctor will give you an examination.
c. I see. You should come to the hospital soon.
d. Please wait and I'll check with the doctor.

Vocabulary

stomachache /stʌ́məkèɪk/ 腹痛 **stabbing** /stǽbɪŋ/ 突き刺すような
disease /dɪzíːz/ 病気 **ulcer** /ʌ́lsər/ 潰瘍 **distended** /dɪsténdɪd/ 膨張した
due date /djúː dèɪt/ 出産予定日 **cough** /kɔːf, kɔf/ せきをする
phlegm /flem/ 痰

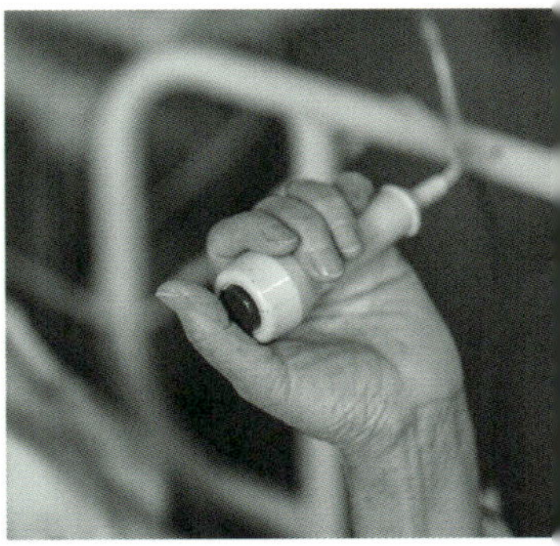

C ペアになって、患者と看護師のセリフを声に出して言ってみましょう。看護師役は前のページを参考にして、英語の言い回しを考えてみましょう。

1

Nurse
今日、ご気分はいかがですか。

Patient
Not very well. I have a stomachache. When I'm hungry, I feel a stabbing pain. I'm really worried about a serious disease. I'm afraid I might have an ulcer.

Nurse
胃が痛いのですね？　医師が検査をします。

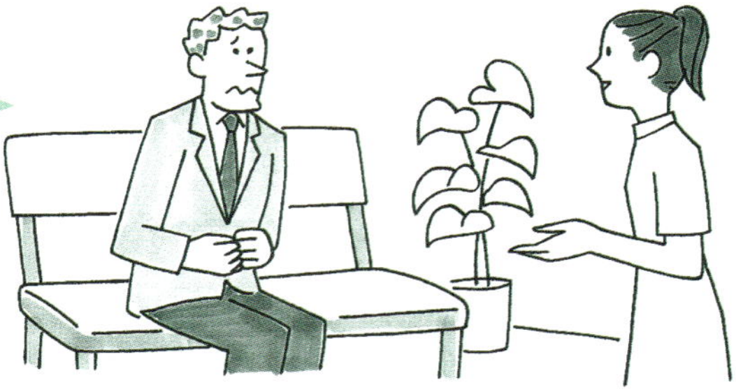

2

N 今日、ご気分はいかがですか。

P Not good. My abdomen feels distended. My due date is one month away. When I went for my checkup last week, the doctor said nothing is wrong. But this morning, I feel something is wrong.

N わかりました。すぐに病院へ来てください。

3

N 今日、ご気分はいかがですか。

P I feel much better today. The longer I stay in bed, the weaker my legs are getting day by day. I feel a little pain when I stand up. But I want to be able to practice walking soon.

N 待っていてくださいね。医師に確認します。

4

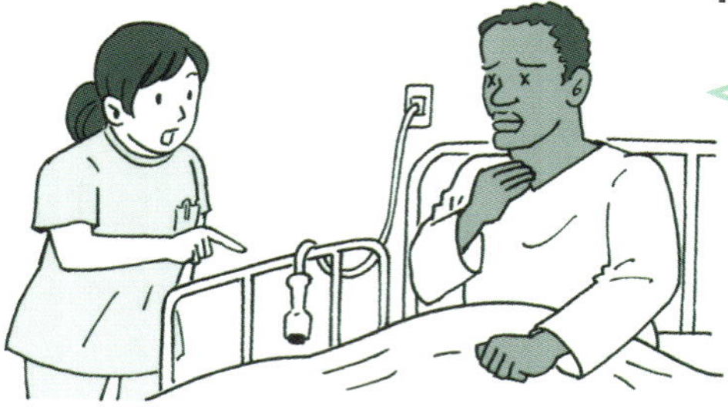

N 今日、ご気分はいかがですか。

P I don't feel very well. I kept coughing for hours last night. It took a long time to get the phlegm from my throat. I couldn't fall asleep until 3:00 in the morning.

N 必要なときはコールボタンを押してください。

Let's Read

A-27

以下の文章はアメリカ国立がん研究所（National Cancer Institute）が、がん患者を支援するために発行している、痛みの管理についての患者向けのパンフレットの一部です。患者が痛みについて医療従事者に伝えるときには何に気をつけたらよいのでしょうか。

Talking about your pain.

The first step in getting your pain under control is talking honestly about it. Try to talk with your health care team and your loved ones about what you are feeling. This means telling them:

- Where you have pain
- What it feels like (sharp, dull, throbbing, constant, burning, or shooting)
- How strong your pain is
- How long it lasts
- What lessens your pain or makes it worse
- When it happens (what time of day, what you're doing, and what's going on)
- If it gets in the way of daily activities

Describe and rate your pain.

You will be asked to describe and rate your pain. This provides a way to assess your pain threshold and measure how well your pain control plan is working.

Your doctor may ask you to describe your pain in a number of ways. A pain scale is the most common way. The scale uses the numbers 0 to 10, where 0 is no pain, and 10 is the worst. You can also use words to describe pain, like pinching, stinging, or aching. Some doctors show their patients a series of faces and ask them to point to the face that best describes how they feel.

Vocabulary

6 **throbbing** ずきずきする
10 **lessen** …を減らす
13 **get in the way of** …の妨げとなる
16 **threshold** 発端

No matter how you or your doctor keep track of your pain, make sure that you do it the same way each time. You also need to talk about any new pain you feel.

It may help to keep a record of your pain. Some people use a pain diary or journal. Others create a list or a computer spreadsheet. Choose the way that works best for you.

Your record could list:

- When you take pain medicine
- The name and dose of the medicine you're taking
- Any side effects you have
- How much the medicine lowers the pain level
- How long the pain medicine works
- Other pain relief methods you use to control your pain
- Any activity that is affected by pain, or makes it better or worse
- Things that you can't do at all because of the pain

Share your record with your health care team. It can help them figure out how helpful your pain medicines are, or if they need to change your pain control plan.

Here are some ways your health care team may ask you to describe or rate your pain: https://www.cancer.gov/publications/patient-education/paincontrol.pdf

Vocabulary

30 **spreadsheet** 集計表
33 **dose** 服用量
34 **side effect** 副作用

Wong-Baker FACES® Pain Rating Scale

A がん患者が痛みの管理をするためには何が重要でしょうか。空欄を埋めて要約文を完成させましょう。

1. 痛みについて医師に (1　　　　　　　) に伝えること。伝えるべき 7 つのことは、(2　　　　　　)、(3　　　　　　)、(4　　　　　　)、(5　　　　　　)、痛みを軽減または悪化させること、(6　　　　　　)、日常生活を妨げるかどうか。
2. 医師は、さまざまな方法で痛みを説明するように求めるかもしれないが、(7　　　　　　) スケールが最も一般的である。(8　　　　　　) で表現してもよいし、(9　　　　　　) のスケールを使う医師もいる。(10　　　　　　) 方法で説明することが重要で、(11　　　　　　) 感じた痛みがあれば伝える必要がある。
3. さまざまな方法で痛みを記録しておくのは大切だが、(12　　　　　　) 方法を選び、その記録を医療従事者と (13　　　　　　) ことも大切である。

B 本文に出てきた痛みを表す形容詞です。一致する日本語の意味を選び、記号を (　　) に入れましょう。

1. sharp pain (　　)
2. dull pain (　　)
3. throbbing pain (　　)
4. constant pain (　　)
5. burning pain (　　)
6. shooting pain (　　)
7. pinching pain (　　)
8. stinging pain (　　)
9. aching pain (　　)

a. ビーンと走るような痛み（電撃痛）
b. 鈍い痛み
c. ひりひりする（灼けるような）痛み
d. 継続する痛み
e. つねられるような痛み
f. 急性の鋭い痛み
g. 慢性のうずく痛み（疼痛）
h. ずきずきする痛み（拍動痛）
i. チクッと（チクチク）する痛み（刺痛）

Let's Write

質問に答えてみましょう。

Q. Do you want to use a Faces Pain Scale? Why or why not?

A. ______________________________

____

UNIT 5

Could you fill in this medical questionnaire?

この問診票にご記入いただけますか

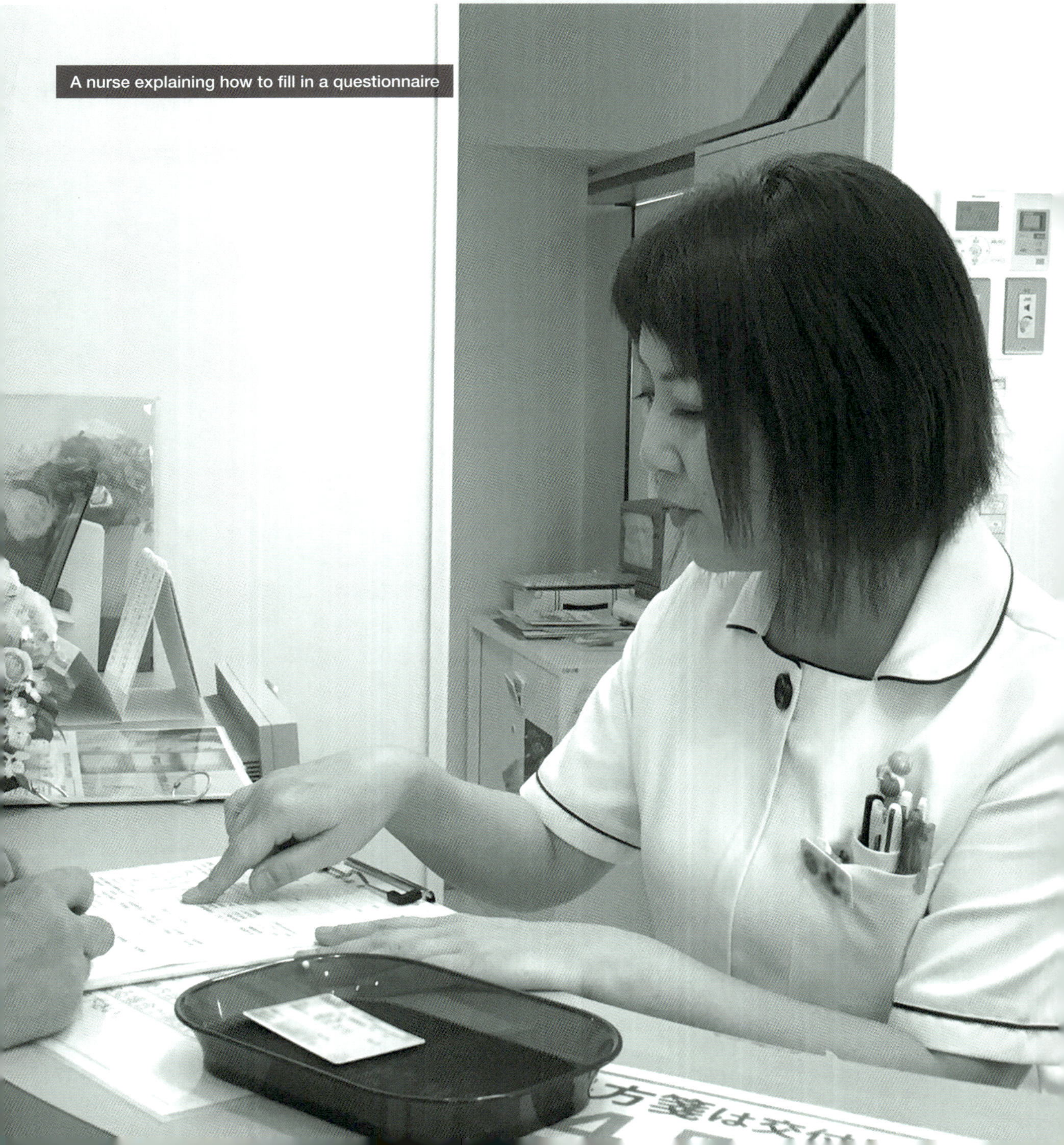

A nurse explaining how to fill in a questionnaire

外国人患者が問診票を記入する手伝いをするときや、症状や病歴について聞くときには、今までに見たことがないような医療専門用語が必要になります。問診票に出てくる症状や病名を表す英単語を覚え、さらに患者とのやりとりに必要な英語表現も覚えてどんな患者ともコミュニケーションがとれる看護師になりましょう。

Dialog

A-28

Nurse

Patient

Nurse: Could you fill in this medical questionnaire?

Patient: Well, I can't read Japanese at all.

Nurse: All right. I think I can help you. What is the problem today?

Patient: I have a squeezing pain in my chest.

Nurse: Have you ever had any serious diseases?

Patient: I had appendicitis five years ago.

Vocabulary

medical questionnaire /médɪk(ə)l kwèstʃənéər/ 問診票 **squeezing** /skwíːzɪŋ/ しめつけられるような
appendicitis /əpèndəsáɪtəs/ 虫垂炎 **hospitalize** /hɑ́(:)spɪt(ə)làɪz/ …を入院させる

A-29

Variations

- どんな症状ですか。 What is the symptom like?
- 病歴を教えていただけますか。 May I ask you about your medical history?
- 今までに手術を受けたことはありますか。 Have you ever had an operation?
- 今までに入院したことはありますか。 Have you ever been hospitalized?
- お薬を飲んでいらっしゃいますか。 Are you taking any medication?

Vocabulary Building

A-30

病名１（内科・消化器系・循環器系）

病名とその説明が一致するカードを選び、その記号を ▢ に入れましょう。また、病名を日本語で空欄に書きましょう。

1	hypertension [ ]	
2	diabetes [ ]	
3	cancer [ ]	
4	ulcer [ ]	
5	hepatitis [ ]	
6	heart attack [ ]	
7	stroke [ ]	
8	pneumonia [ ]	
9	appendicitis [ ]	
10	tuberculosis [ ]	
11	asthma [ ]	

A a very dangerous medical condition in which the heart suddenly stops working properly

B a serious disease of the lungs with inflammation and difficulty in breathing

C a sore area on your skin or inside your body that may bleed or produce poisonous substances

D a very serious disease in which cells in one part of the body start to grow in a way that is not normal

E an illness in which your appendix swells and causes pain

F a serious infectious disease that affects many parts of your body, especially your lungs

G a medical condition that causes difficulties in breathing

H a serious disease in which there is too much sugar in your blood

I a sudden illness in part of the brain which can cause loss of movement in parts of the body

J a medical condition in which your blood pressure is too high

K a disease of the liver that causes fever and makes your skin yellow

Let's Listen

A-31 ▶ 34

A 4人の患者と看護師の会話を聞き、患者の病歴についての key words を英語で書き取りましょう。また、その内容を key words から推測して日本語で書いてみましょう。

	key words	病歴
1		
2		
3		
4		

B 同じ会話をもう1度聞きましょう。それぞれの患者の答えを導く適切な質問を枠内から選び、記号で答えましょう。そして意味を考えながら、暗記するまで何度も読んでみましょう。

1 ＿＿＿　2 ＿＿＿　3 ＿＿＿　4 ＿＿＿

a. Have you ever had any serious illnesses?
b. Have you ever had any serious injuries?
c. Have you ever had an operation?
d. Have you ever been hospitalized?

Vocabulary

myoma /maɪóʊmə/ 筋腫　**uterus** /júːt(ə)rəs/ 子宮
period /píəriəd/ 生理　**anemic** /əníːmɪk/ 貧血の
Caesarean section /sɪzéəriən sékʃ(ə)n/ 帝王切開
neck brace /nek breɪs/ 首の固定具

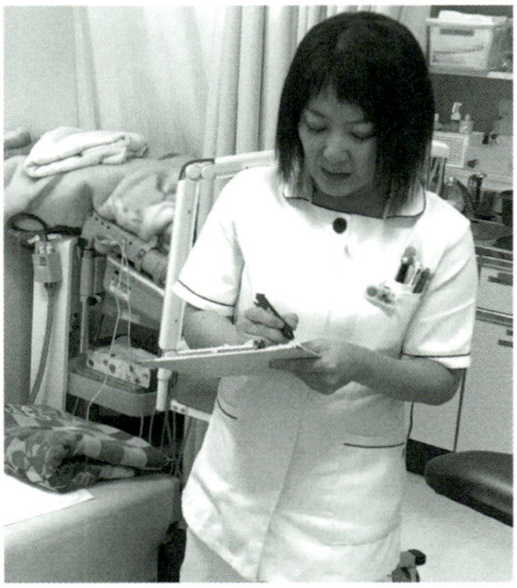

C ペアになって、患者と看護師のセリフを声に出して言ってみましょう。看護師役は前のページを参考にして、英語の言い回しを考えてみましょう。

1

今までに何か大きな病気をしたことはありますか。
Yes. I suffered from a myoma of the uterus. It caused heavy bleeding during my period. I became severely anemic.

2

今までに手術を受けたことはありますか。
Yes. I broke my left leg when I went skiing. I had an operation at the hospital near the ski slope.

3

今までに入院をしたことはありますか。
Yes. I had a Caesarean section when my first son was born. I was in the hospital for two weeks.

4

今までに何か大きなけがをしたことはありますか。

Yes. I hurt my neck in a car accident when I was 21 years old. I had to wear a neck brace for three months.

Let's Read

A-35

この文章を書いた看護師は、初めはあまり本気で人の世話をしようと考えていたわけではありませんでした。ところが、入院先で見た白髪まじりの看護師からプロとしての大切な態度を学びました。それは、忙しい毎日の仕事の中で、１人の患者の要求にたった５分間だけでも集中してあげることでした。

Touchy–Feely Stuff

In 1977, while in nursing school, I was assigned to write an essay entitled "Inspiration, Aspiration, Vocation—Why I Want to Become a Nurse." This title suggested that motivations stronger than mine were in favor at the school.

Job security and a living wage—not a burning desire to care for the sick—drew me to nursing. I wrote about Anne, a hospital roommate I had had when I'd undergone an operation. Anne had suffered from a neurological disease.

The only medical professional I saw who responded appropriately to Anne's complaint of shoulder pain was a gray-haired nurse. She would perform her tasks—neuro check, blood pressure, meds—and adjust the medical machinery. Then she would fold her hands and ask Anne,

Vocabulary

- title **touchy-feely** 感傷的な
- 2 **aspiration** 熱望
- **vocation** 職業
- 3 **motivation** 動機
- 5 **burning** 熱烈な
- 7 **undergo** …を経験する
- 8 **neurological** 神経系の
- 12 **med** = medicine

"What do we need to do today?" She used the term "we" literally—meaning, how could they both make Anne more comfortable?

I watched her massage Anne's back and listened to their conversation, watching how she became Anne's trusted friend. I wondered, "How hard can it be to focus for five minutes on the needs of a patient?" I was watching the art of nursing. And with the grace of a skilled professional, Anne's nurse made it look simple.

In nursing school, however, I was overwhelmed by how much I didn't know. By that time, I had decided that the touchy-feely stuff was all well and good, but I needed to learn the symptoms of diseases first.

I was not a good student in nursing school. But I thought that someday I would become that nurse who calmed the hard working day by folding her hands and listening to her patients.

One month after graduation, I found a job. On the first day, I faced a ward of 32 severely handicapped patients. I felt like a frightened outsider. There was a patient named Daisy. I tried to give her medicine. She glared at me and clenched her teeth. I looked at the aide helplessly. She told me to always say hello to my patients before I treated them. So I repeated "hello" until Daisy narrowed her eyes and gave me a near smile.

She took her meds, but giving her the treatment was difficult, too. I felt I was almost useless much of that day, but my gray-haired muse kept pulling me back to solid ground. Sometimes I snarled at her saintlike image, but it always restored my composure when I interacted with patients.

Vocabulary

21 **skilled** 熟練した
23 **overwhelm** …を圧倒する
32 **ward** 病棟
33 **outsider** 部外者
34 **glare** …をじっとにらむ
clench …をくいしばる
35 **aide** 助手
41 **muse** 女神
42 **snarl** どなる
saintlike 聖人のような
43 **restore** …を取り戻す
composure 平静
interact 交わる

A 本文の内容と一致するものに T (True) を、一致しないものには F (False) を書きましょう。

1. ( ) The writer wanted to be a nurse because she really wanted to care for the sick.
2. ( ) In an assigned essay, the writer wrote about Anne, her hospital roommate.
3. ( ) The gray-haired nurse would ask Anne, "What do I need to do today?"
4. ( ) The writer's first job was not very difficult.
5. ( ) When the writer cared for patients, she often remembered how the gray-haired nurse had treated her patients.

B 筆者がベテランの看護師を見て、心を動かされたのはなぜでしょうか。2 つの点でまとめましょう。

1. 患者との向き合い方

____

____

____

2. 看護の技術

____

Let's Write

質問に答えてみましょう。

Q. Describe what your ideal nurse is like.

A. ______________________________

____

UNIT 6 Take the elevator, please.

行き先を案内しましょう

Nurses in a nurses station

大きい病院では、受付・診察室・検査室などがあり、症状によって診察を受ける科もいくつかに分かれています。外国人患者がそういう病院を訪れたら、一体どこへ行けばいいのかとても不安に感じることでしょう。どこへ行くべきなのかを英語で分かりやすく説明することを学びましょう。

Dialog

A-36

Nurse

Patient

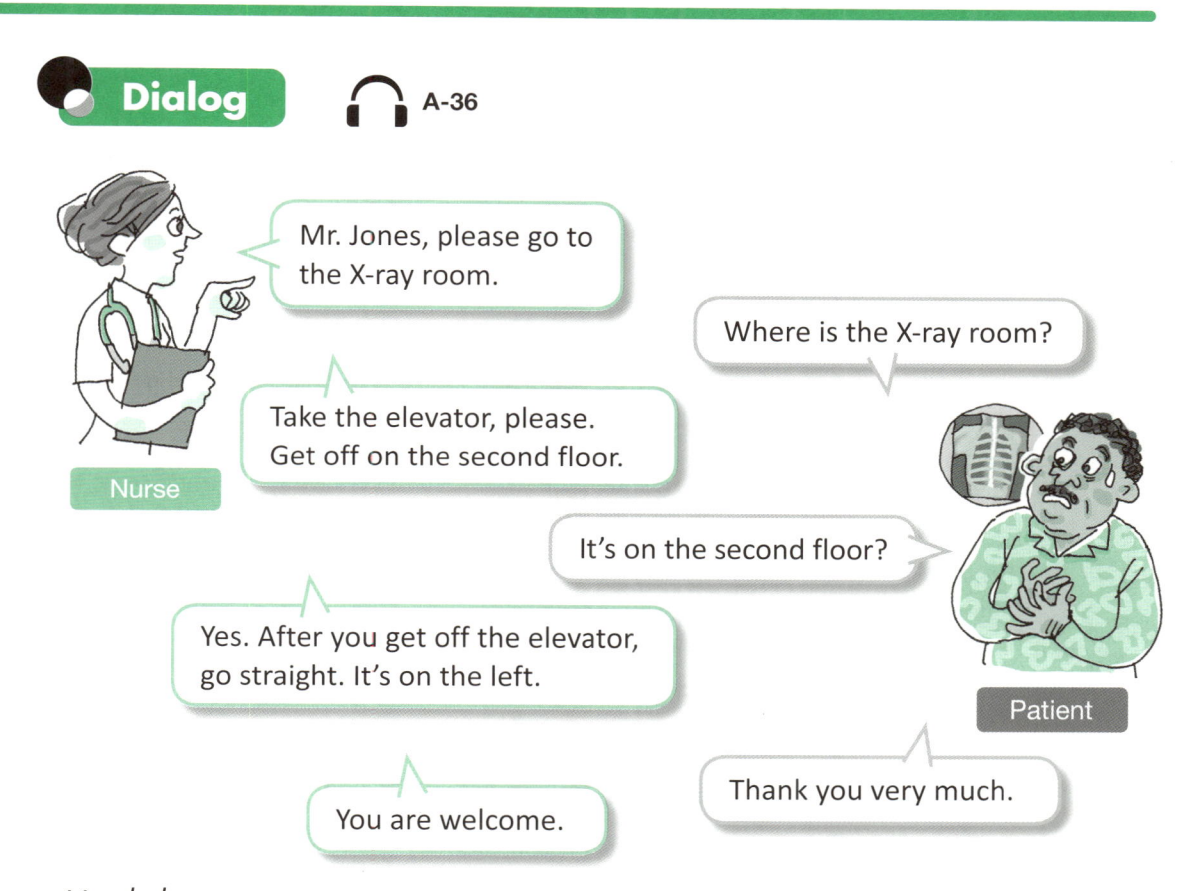

Nurse: Mr. Jones, please go to the X-ray room.

Patient: Where is the X-ray room?

Nurse: Take the elevator, please. Get off on the second floor.

Patient: It's on the second floor?

Nurse: Yes. After you get off the elevator, go straight. It's on the left.

Patient: Thank you very much.

Nurse: You are welcome.

Vocabulary

X-ray /éksrèɪ/ エックス線

A-37

Variations

- エスカレーターをご利用ください。 **Take the escalator, please.**
- 脳神経外科はお手洗いの向かいにあります。 **Neurosurgery is across from the restrooms.**
- 泌尿器科は小児科の隣です。 **Urology is next to Pediatrics.**
- エレベーターは廊下の突き当たりです。 **The elevator is at the end of the hall.**
- 喫茶室は地下です。 **The coffee shop is in the basement.**

Vocabulary Building

A-38

病名 2（精神科・小児科・外科・整形外科・耳鼻科・その他）

傷病名とその説明が一致するカードを選び、その記号を [ ] に入れましょう。また、病名を日本語で空欄に書きましょう。

1	fracture [ ]	
2	dislocation [ ]	
3	sprain [ ]	
4	burn [ ]	
5	chicken pox [ ]	
6	measles [ ]	
7	neurosis [ ]	
8	dementia [ ]	
9	hay fever [ ]	
10	myoma [ ]	
11	tooth decay [ ]	

A an infectious illness in which you have a fever and small red spots on your face and body

B a mental illness that makes someone unreasonably worried and frightened

C a benign tumor composed of muscular tissue

D severe impairment or loss of intellectual capacity and personality integration

E an infectious illness which causes a slight fever and eruption of blisters on your skin

F a break, rupture, or crack, especially in bone or cartilage

G the formation of cavities in the teeth by the action of bacteria

H a stretched or torn ligament caused by falling or twisting

I a medical condition, like a bad cold that is caused by breathing in pollen

J displacement of a bone from its normal position, especially at a joint

K an injury caused by fire, heat, the light of the sun, or acid

Let's Listen

A-39 ▶ 42

A 4 人の患者と看護師の会話を聞き、患者の質問の key words を英語で書き取りましょう。また、その内容を key words から推測して日本語で書いてみましょう。

	key words	質問
1		
2		
3		
4		

B 同じ会話をもう 1 度聞きましょう。それぞれの患者への適切な指示を枠内から選び、記号で答えましょう。そして意味を考えながら、暗記するまで何度も読んでみましょう。

1 ____ 2 ____ 3 ____ 4 ____

a. Please take it to the outside pharmacy. Go out of the front entrance. You can see the pharmacy across the street.
b. Go straight. It's on the left at the end of the hall.
c. It's on the second floor. Please take the escalator. When you get off, turn right. It's on the right.
d. Go straight and turn right at the next corner. Then you can find the shop in front of you.

Vocabulary

urine test /júərən test/ 尿検査
lab = laboratory /læb/ 検査室
diaper /dá(ɪ)əpə/ おむつ
pharmacy /fáːrməsi/ 薬局
prescription /prɪskrípʃ(ə)n/ 処方箋

C ペアになって、患者と看護師のセリフを声に出して言ってみましょう。看護師役は下の案内図と前のページを参考にして、英語の言い回しを考えてみましょう。

Patient

1 I have a terrible toothache. Where is Dentistry located?

2 I was told to take a urine test. Could you tell me how to get to the Urine Lab?

3 I need to buy adult diapers for my mother. Where is the shop?

4 There is no pharmacy inside the hospital. Where shall I take this prescription?

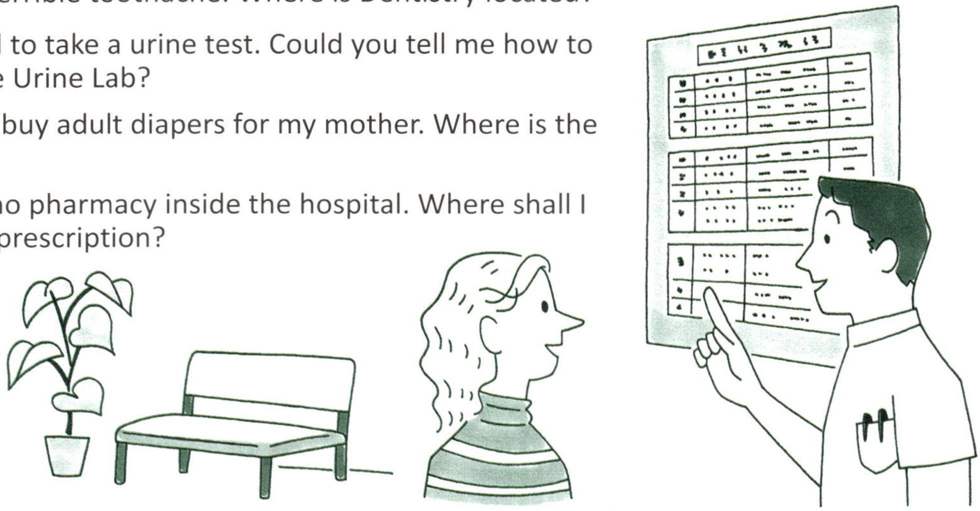

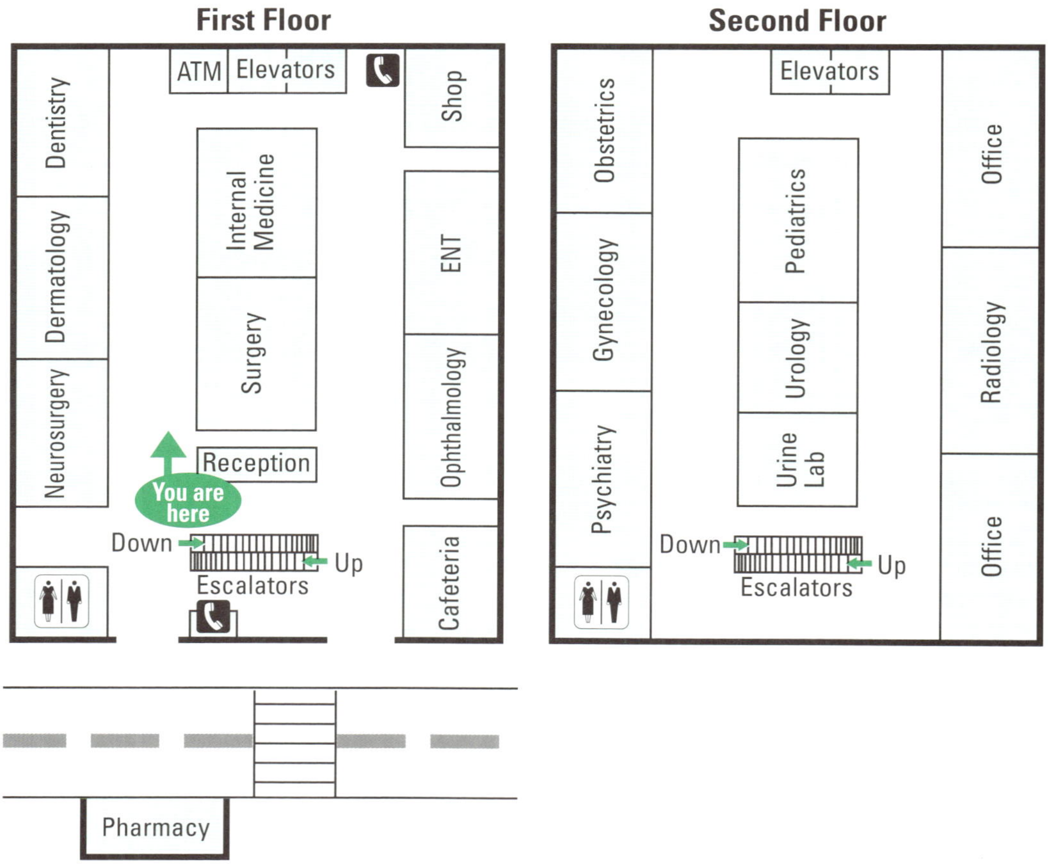

Let's Read

A-43

人間が地球以外に住むことができる場所として、今、考えられるのは火星ではないでしょうか。火星に人間が住むようになったら、当然、健康状態を管理することができる看護師が必要とされるでしょう。「火星で働く看護師になってみたら」という記事がアメリカの看護師向けの学術誌（*American Journal of Nursing*）に載りました。あなたも考えてみてはどうでしょうか。

A Nurse on Mars? Why Not?

In this century, people in environments beyond Earth will require health care. Nurses' contributions need not be restricted to Earth; their skills are of value in space as well. With space exploration proceeding at such a steady pace, now may be a good time to start thinking about working in a space station on Mars.

The National Aeronautics and Space Administration (NASA) employs both nurses and physicians for ground-based monitoring of the health of more than 400 astronauts. The number of "flight nurses," those working directly with flight crews, is still small, but opportunities can be expected to increase significantly over the next two decades.

NASA's flight nurses also coordinate dietary and fitness services. At the first sign of physical discomfort, an astronaut first contacts a nurse, who gives appropriate treatment. Other nurses are employed as support staff for more specific treatment.

Currently NASA's nurses are not employed on flights in the astronaut program. Physicians and other scientists handle any onboard medical needs on space missions. But this is not to say nurses will never be able to perform onboard service. Wherever there are patients, there will be nurses.

Vocabulary

title **Mars** 火星
4 **exploration** 探査
7- **National Aeronautics and Space Administration (NASA)** アメリカ航空宇宙局
8 **physician** 医師
9 **astronaut** 宇宙飛行士
13 **coordinate** …を調整する
fitness 健康
20 **onboard** 機内での

Today's nursing students will likely have career options in space nursing during their lifetimes. Knowledge of space health hazards such as decompression and radiation exposure, self-care measures to prevent bone loss and muscle deconditioning, and knowledge of sterile procedures in microgravity are a few topics that may one day be nursing fundamentals.

Space travelers who experience close calls with death, serious accidents, or the death of crewmembers would need help with the resultant grief and loss. Isolation and loneliness have been reported by astronauts. Nurses with backgrounds in psychiatric nursing or additional education in human development, psychology, and sociology will be especially valuable.

Though none of the nursing programs include courses concerning nursing in space, nursing educators and theorists have put forth new ideas about health care in space. The range and extent of health-related risks and the unique challenges promised by travel in space suggest that nurses can make important contributions.

Vocabulary

25 **hazard** 危険
decompression 減圧
25- **radiation exposure** 放射線被曝
26- **muscle deconditioning** 筋力の低下
27 **sterile** 無菌の
28 **microgravity** 微小重力
30 **close call** 危機一髪
32 **resultant** 結果として生じる
grief 悲痛
isolation 孤立
35 **sociology** 社会学
38 **theorist** 理論家
39 **put forth** …を提唱する

A 本文の内容と一致するものに T (True) を、一致しないものには F (False) を書きましょう。

1. (　　　) NASA のフライト・ナースは現在 400 人以上いる。
2. (　　　) 宇宙飛行士の健康管理を行うフライト・ナースは、特に宇宙飛行士の減量に努めなければならない。
3. (　　　) 今後、看護師が宇宙船に搭乗することもある。
4. (　　　) 火星では生物の存在が確認されていないので、無菌処置をする必要はない。
5. (　　　) 火星で勤務する看護師を選考する際、看護学以外の学識を多く持つ人ほど待遇がよくなる。

B 火星の環境が地球と異なる点を英語で 3 つ挙げましょう。

1. ____________________
2. ____________________
3. ____________________

Let's Write

質問に答えてみましょう。

Q. Do you want to go to space as a nurse? Why or why not?

A. ____________________

____

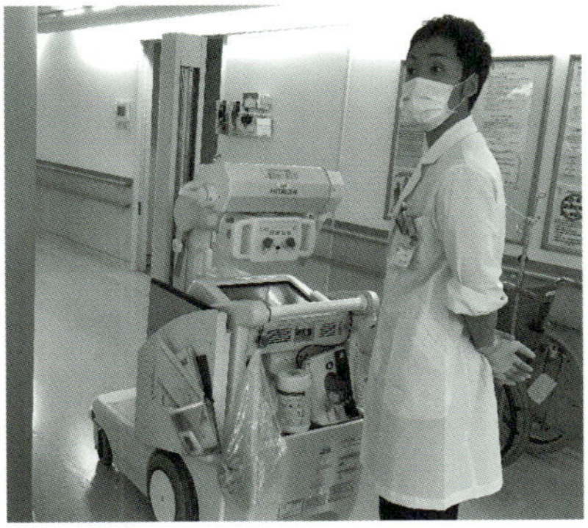

UNIT 7

What are your symptoms?

症状を尋ねましょう

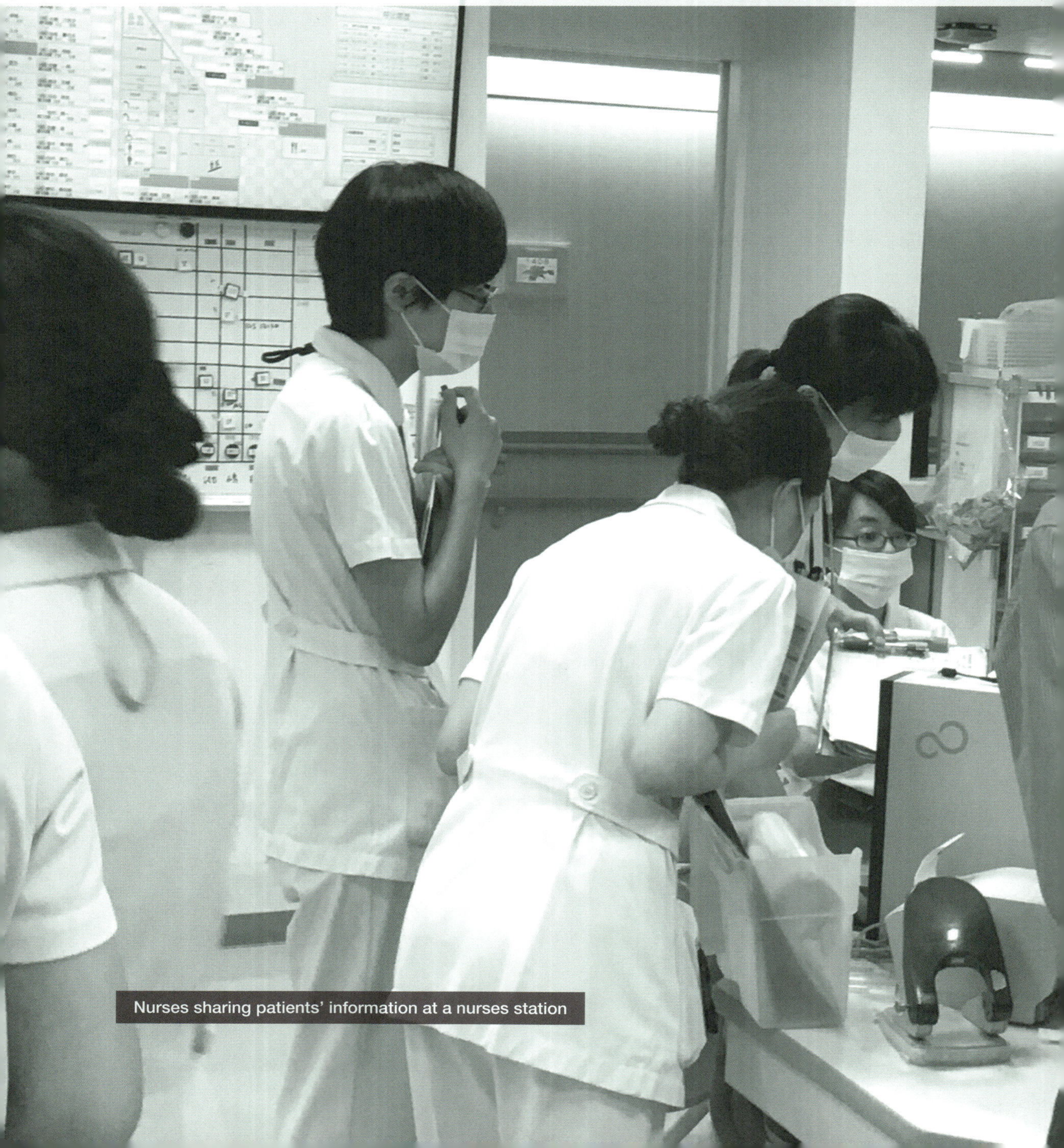

Nurses sharing patients' information at a nurses station

医療現場で活躍している看護師が答えてくれたアンケートによると、英語で一番必要だと思う表現は、「症状を尋ねる」ことでした。さまざまな症状の尋ね方を学びましょう。これらの表現をあなたも必要とするはずです。

Dialog

A-44

Nurse

What are your symptoms today?

I have diarrhea. I have had it three times since last night.

Do you have a fever?

Maybe. I feel chilly.

OK. Let's take your temperature. How is your appetite?

Poor. I feel nauseous. I threw up once this morning.

Patient

Vocabulary

symptom /sím(p)təm/ 症状 **diarrhea** /dà(ɪ)əríːə/ 下痢 **chilly** /tʃíli/ 寒気がする
nauseous /nɔ́ːʃəs/ 吐き気がする

A-45

Variations

- どうなさいましたか。 **What seems to be the problem?**
  What is the problem today?
  What's the matter?
- どんな症状ですか。 **What symptoms have you noticed?**
  What symptoms do you have?

Vocabulary Building

A-46

症状１（頭部）

症状名と一致するイラストを選び、その記号を　　に入れましょう。また、症状名を日本語で空欄に書きましょう。

1	headache		
2	dizziness		
3	depression		
4	insomnia		
5	eye mucus / eye discharge		
6	runny nose		
7	sneezing		
8	sore throat		
9	earache		
10	stiff neck		

a

b

c

d

e

f

g

h

i

j

Let's Listen

A-47 ▶ 50

A 4 人の患者と看護師の会話を聞き、患者の症状についての key words を英語で書き取りましょう。また、その内容を key words から推測して日本語で書いてみましょう。

	key words	どこが、どのような症状か
1		
2		
3		
4		

B 同じ会話をもう 1 度聞きましょう。それぞれの患者に与える適切な説明や指示を枠内から選び、記号で答えましょう。そして意味を考えながら、暗記するまで何度も読んでみましょう。

1 ____ 2 ____ 3 ____ 4 ____

a. We'll do a urine test. Please go to the examination room.
b. Please wait for a few minutes. The doctor will see you soon.
c. Please talk to the doctor.
d. I will take your pulse and blood pressure. Please lie down and try not to move.

Vocabulary

depressed /dɪprést/ 気分が沈んだ
blood pressure /blʌ́d prèʃər/ 血圧
burning /bə́ːrnɪŋ/ ヒリヒリとした
pulse /pʌls/ 脈拍
swallow /swɑ́(ː)loʊ/ 飲み込む
urinate /júərənèɪt/ 排尿する

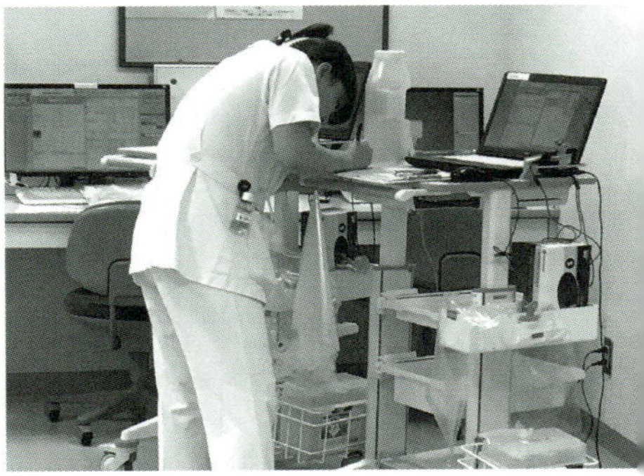

C ペアになって、患者と看護師のセリフを声に出して言ってみましょう。看護師役は前のページを参考にして、英語の言い回しを考えてみましょう。

1

Nurse
どうなさいましたか。

Patient
I have a bad headache. I often wake up at night. I have so many things to do these days.
I sometimes feel depressed.

Nurse
医師と話をしてください。

2

N どんな症状ですか。

P I have chest pains. When I came back from a walk, I suddenly felt a sharp pain in my chest.

N 脈拍と血圧を測ります。横になって動かないでください。

3

N どうなさいましたか。

P I have a sore throat. It was really swollen when I checked with a mirror. It hurts when I swallow.

N 少しお待ちください。医師がすぐ診ます。

4

N どんな症状ですか。

P I have a burning pain when I urinate. And I have to use the toilet frequently.

N 尿検査をします。検査室へ行ってください。

Let's Read

A-51

看護師である筆者は、交通事故で入院した病院で何人もの看護師に出会います。それぞれの看護師は、それぞれの持ち場で常に患者に寄り添っています。タイトルに “Nurses Know” とありますが、看護師の知っていること（看護師が身につけていること）とは何でしょうか。

Nurses Know

It happened back in 1976. While I was driving home from the Visiting Nurse Association, a cement truck lost control and hit me broadside. I was lifted onto a stretcher and transported to a nearby ED.

In the ED, a nurse named Sheila helped move me to a gurney. While I was X-rayed lying down, sitting on a stool, and standing, I heard Sheila's voice from the hallway. “She could have a spinal injury. Don't move her from the gurney.” Thank God, I thought. *Nurses know basic first aid guidelines.*

Back in the ED, the physician told me, “The X-rays show a fracture of a cervical vertebra. A week or 10 days in traction and then a neck brace for a couple of months should do it.” After Sheila applied the stiff collar and used sandbags to stabilize my head, I was taken to the neurology unit.

I was met by a young resident. “I'm going to drill little holes in each side of your head to set up the traction.” I gasped. “How many times have you done this before?” He didn't answer, but kept setting things up. I looked at Joanne, the nurse. “Mike,” Joanne said kindly, “Let's page the senior resident.” We waited for the senior resident, and then they got to work. I cringed at the sound of the drill boring through my skull, and as the weights were attached to the tongs, tears filled my eyes. But Joanne was there. “Try to relax,” she

Vocabulary

2 **Visiting Nurse Association** 訪問看護師協会
3 **broadside** 側面に
4 **transport** …を搬送する
ED 救急科（= Emergency Department）
6 **gurney** 台車付き担架
8 **spinal** 脊椎の
11 **cervical vertebra** 頸椎
traction 牽引
13 **collar** 首の固定具
14 **stabilize** …を安定させる
15 **resident** 研修医
17 **gasp** 息をのむ
19 **page** …を呼び出す
21 **cringe at …** （恐怖などで身がすくむ
bore 突き通す
22 **skull** 頭蓋骨
tongs トング（はさむ道具）

said. "You're doing very well." *Nurses know how to act as advocates, how to reassure patients.*

The next day a neurosurgeon examined me and suggested surgery to fuse the C6 vertebra with a bone graft from my hip. After talking it over with my family, I consented. The morning of the surgery, a technician came to transport me, and began removing the weights from my head. "The weights have to stay on," I said, and asked for the nurse. The nurse came in and insisted the weights stay in place for the transfer. *Nurses know how to keep patients safe.*

After the surgery I had to lie flat in bed for another week. I was bored and discouraged, but the nurses were there. A favorite nurse was Karen. "Another few days and you'll have your body cast," she said. "Then you'll be able to get up and walk." *Nurses know how to provide emotional support.*

Finally my stitches were removed, and I was taken to the cast room for the application of the Minerva jacket. Afterward, back in my room, I ran my fingers over an oily braid sticking up from the opening in the top of the cast. My hair hadn't been washed for two weeks. Karen came and asked if I wanted a shampoo. "I'd love that," I said. When Karen finished washing my hair, she braided it again into a single, clean plait. "That feels wonderful," I said. *Nurses know how important personal comfort is.*

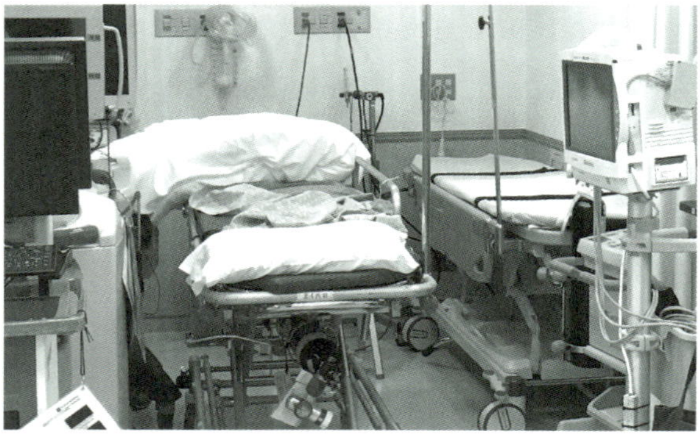

Vocabulary

25 **reassure** …を安心させる
27 **fuse** …を結合させる
C6 vertebra 第6頸椎
bone graft 骨移植片
35 **discouraged** 落胆した
37 **body cast** 体幹ギプス
39 **stitches** 縫合の糸
40 **Minerva jacket** ミネルバジャケット
42 **braid** 編んだ髪
46 **plait** おさげ

A 体験談の中に登場する医療従事者の名称を日本語に訳して、表を完成させましょう。

英語	日本語
physician	
resident	（専門分野の）研修医
senior resident	上級研修医
neurosurgeon	
technician	

B それぞれの場面で、看護師は何を知っていて筆者のケアをしたのかを、枠内から選び、表を完成させましょう。

看護師	体験談の中の場面	看護師が知っていること
Sheila	エックス線検査中	
Joanne	頭部へのギプス装着時	
Nurse	手術前の移動時	
Karen	手術後	
Karen	手術 2 週間後	

a. 患者のために声を上げること
b. 患者を感情的に支えること
c. 患者の安全を確保する方法
d. 患者を安心させること
e. 体を快適にすることの大切さ
f. 基本的な救急処置の指針

Let's Write

質問に答えてみましょう。

Q. Have you or your family ever been hospitalized? If yes, when and why?

A. ______________________________

____

UNIT 8 Where does it hurt?

痛みの場所を聞きましょう

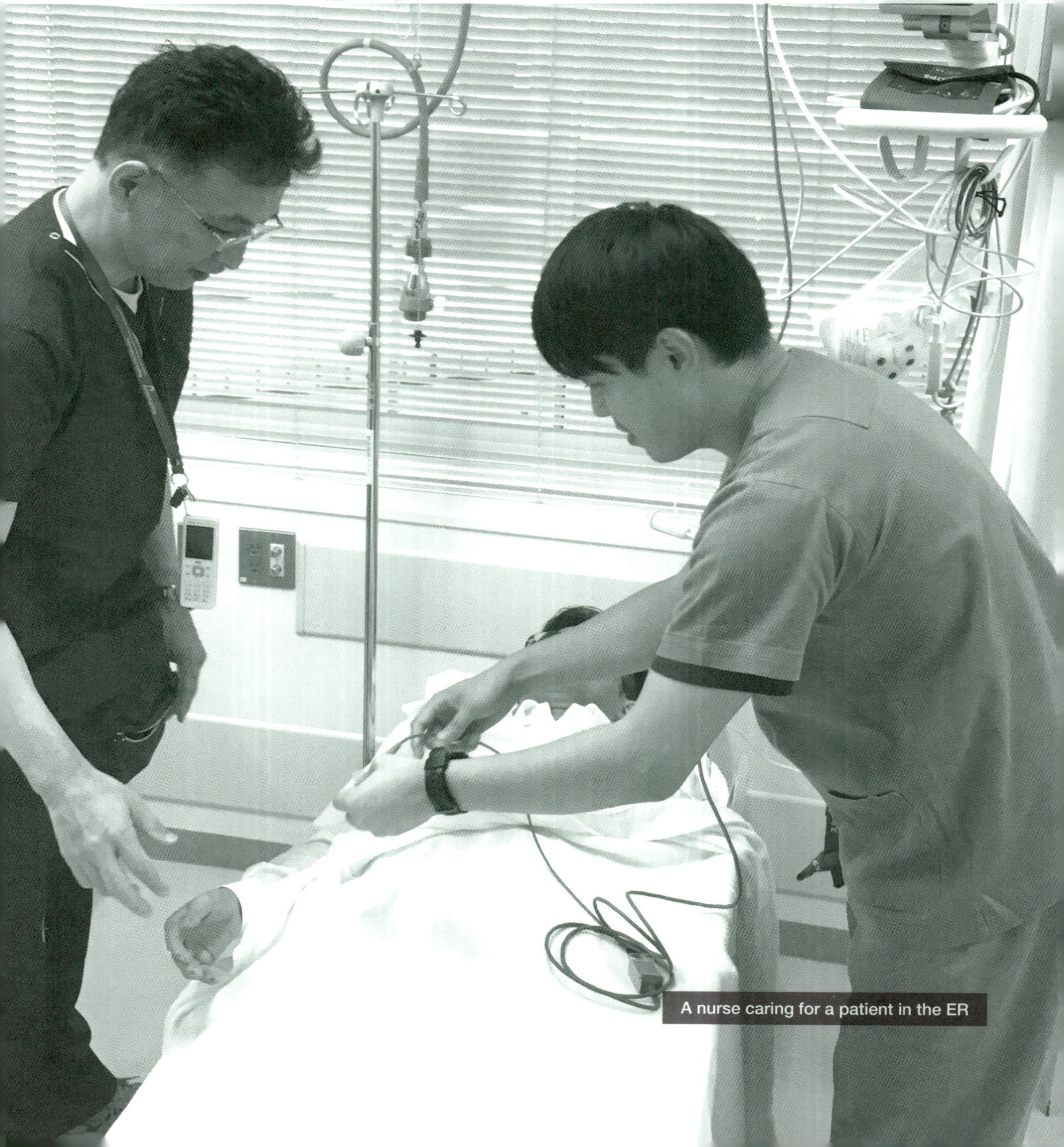

A nurse caring for a patient in the ER

病院を訪れる患者は、何らかの不快な症状や痛みを持って、不安な気持ちを抱えてやってきます。ましてや、それが言葉の違う外国だったらさらに強い不安を感じているはずです。柔らかな声で痛みの場所を聞き、患者の訴えに耳を傾けましょう。そして指示を与えるときは、的確にはっきりと自信を持って英語を口にしましょう。

Dialog

A-52

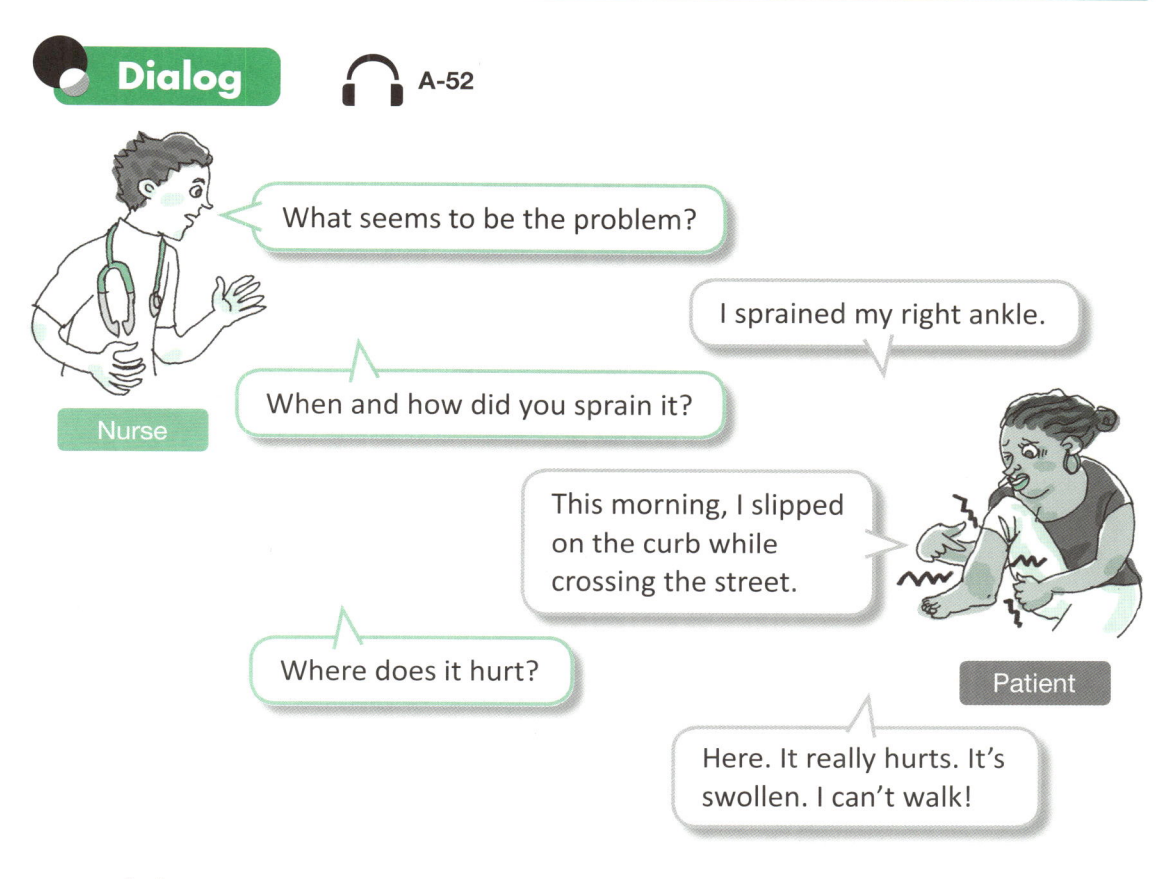

Nurse: What seems to be the problem?

Patient: I sprained my right ankle.

Nurse: When and how did you sprain it?

Patient: This morning, I slipped on the curb while crossing the street.

Nurse: Where does it hurt?

Patient: Here. It really hurts. It's swollen. I can't walk!

Vocabulary

sprain /spreɪn/ …をねんざする　**curb** /kəːrb/（歩道の）縁

A-53

Variations

- どこが痛みますか。 **Where's the pain?** **Where do you feel pain?**
- どこをけがしましたか。 **Where did you hurt yourself?**
- 症状のある部分に○をつけてください。 **Circle the place where you are experiencing the symptom.**

Vocabulary Building

A-54

症状 2（肩から下）

症状名と一致するイラストを選び、その記号を ［　］ に入れましょう。また、症状名を日本語で空欄に書きましょう。

1	cough		
2	chest pain		
3	phlegm		
4	palpitations		
5	lump in the breast		
6	vomiting		
7	constipation		
8	fatigue		
9	abdominal pain		
10	leg cramp		
11	joint pain		

a

b

c

d

e

f

g

h

i

j

k

Let's Listen

A-55 ▶ 58

A 4 人の患者と看護師の会話を聞き、患者の痛みについての key words を英語で書き取りましょう。また、その内容を key words から推測して日本語で書いてみましょう。

	key words	痛みについて
1		
2		
3		
4		

B 同じ会話をもう 1 度聞きましょう。それぞれの患者への適切な説明や指示を枠内から選び、記号で答えましょう。そして意味を考えながら、暗記するまで何度も読んでみましょう。

1 ＿＿＿＿　2 ＿＿＿＿　3 ＿＿＿＿　4 ＿＿＿＿

a. **You will need to have an X-ray.**
b. **We'll do a blood test. Please wait here.**
c. **Please lie on your back or on your side.**
d. **Let me wash your eye.**

Vocabulary

joint /dʒɔɪnt/ 関節　**muddy** /mʌ́di/ 泥だらけの
swollen /swóʊl(ə)n/ 腫れた　**eyelid** /áɪlìd/ まぶた
eye mucus /aɪ mjúːkəs/ 目やに

C ペアになって、患者と看護師のセリフを声に出して言ってみましょう。看護師役は前のページを参考にして、英語の言い回しを考えてみましょう。

1

Nurse
どこが痛みますか。

Patient
When I wake up in the morning, my joints ache. The pain is usually worse on rainy days.

Nurse
血液検査をします。ここでお待ちください。

2

N どこが痛みますか。

P I hurt my lower back. I was playing baseball yesterday. I slipped while running on the muddy ground.

N 仰向けか横向きに寝てください。

3

N どこが痛みますか。

P I went fishing in the river. I slipped on a big rock. When I fell, I sprained my wrist. It really hurts!

N エックス線検査が必要です。

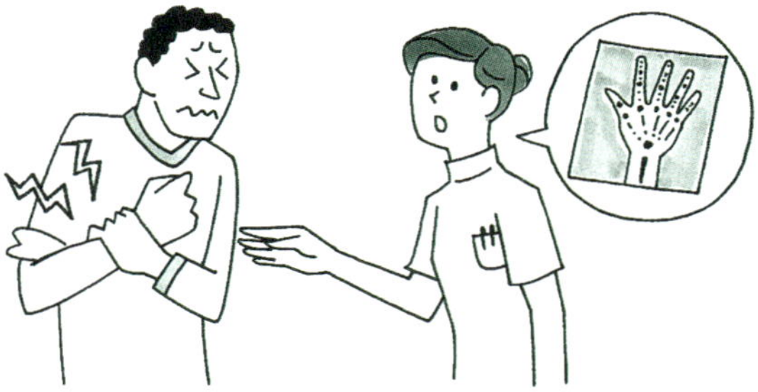

4

N どこが痛みますか。

P I have a swollen eyelid. It is very painful. I have a lot of eye mucus, and I can't see well with my left eye.

N 洗眼しましょう。

Let's Read

A-59

映画紹介

オリバー・サックスという医学博士の実際の体験に基づいて作られたこの映画は、医者、患者と看護師が織りなす素晴らしい人間模様が描かれています。医療や看護、人生について考えさせてくれるでしょう。

AWAKENINGS
（レナードの朝）

Dateline: 1969, The Bronx. Dr. Sayer began working as a neurologist in a chronic care hospital. He met a group of patients, many of whom had spent decades in a strange, frozen state, unable to move. They were given up as hopeless cases. However, Dr. Sayer found out that these patients were survivors of "sleeping-sickness." Helped by some nurses and hospital staff, he tried to find ways to give them appropriate treatment because he believed the patients were normal inside. He treated them with a then-experimental drug, L-dopa. It made the patients come back to life after decades in a stupor. Leonard was one of these patients.

After the miraculous awakening, Leonard said:

"We've got to tell everybody. We've got to remind them how good it is. Read the newspaper. It's all bad. People have forgotten what life is all about. They forgot what it is to be alive. They need to be reminded about what they have and what they can lose. What I feel is the joy of life—the gift of life, and the freedom of life and the wonderment of life."

The patients were at first thrilled about the awakenings. Leonard fell in love with Pola, who was visiting her father in the same hospital. However, the miracle didn't last very long. The serious side effects of L-dopa began to affect Leonard and other patients. He began to develop tics and terrible fits.

Vocabulary

title **awakening** 目覚め
2 **neurologist** 神経科医
chronic 慢性の（⇔ acute 急性の）
9 **then-experimental** 当時実験段階の
11 **stupor** 麻痺状態
12 **miraculous** 奇跡的な
18 **wonderment** 驚き
19 **thrilled** 感動（興奮）して
21 **last** 続く
23 **tic** 顔面筋などの不随意けいれん
fit けいれん、発作

He was depressed by the change. He finally decided to tell Pola not to meet him at the hospital's cafeteria anymore. Pola refused to give up on Leonard and was able to ease the tic by cheek dancing with him. However, Leonard slowly and irreversibly became frozen again.

In the last part of the movie, Dr. Sayer said:

"A miracle for 15 patients and for us, their caretakers. But now we have to adjust to the realities of the miracle. We can hide behind the veil of science and say it was the drug that failed, or that the illness itself had returned, or that the patients were unable to cope with losing decades of their lives. But the reality is we don't know what went wrong any more than we know what went right. What we do know is as the chemical window closed, another awakening took place—that the human spirit is more powerful than any drug. And that is what needs to be nourished—with work, play, friendship, family. These are the things that matter. This is what we had forgotten. The simplest things."

Vocabulary

28 **irreversibly** いや応なく

34 **cope with** …にうまく対処する

39 **nourish** …をはぐくむ

A 本文の内容と一致するものに T (True) を、一致しないものには F (False) を書きましょう。

1. (　　) Dr. Sayer wanted to treat the patients with sleeping-sickness, but no one helped him find appropriate treatment.
2. (　　) After the awakening miraculously happened, Leonard said that people should remember what life is all about.
3. (　　) Leonard was the only patient who began to suffer from side effects caused by L-dopa.
4. (　　) Dr. Sayer concludes that the human spirit is stronger than any medicine.
5. (　　) Fifty patients were cured after taking L-dopa.

Let's Write

質問に答えてみましょう。

Q. What is the greatest joy of your life?

A. ______________________________

____

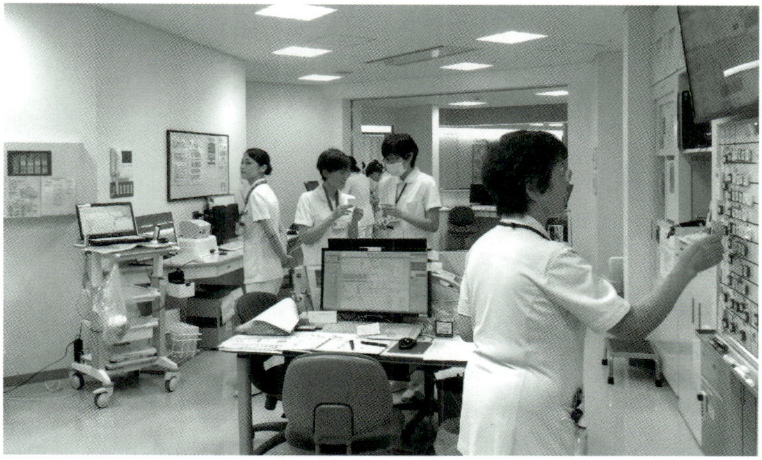

UNIT 9 How long have you had these symptoms?

症状の持続時間を聞きましょう

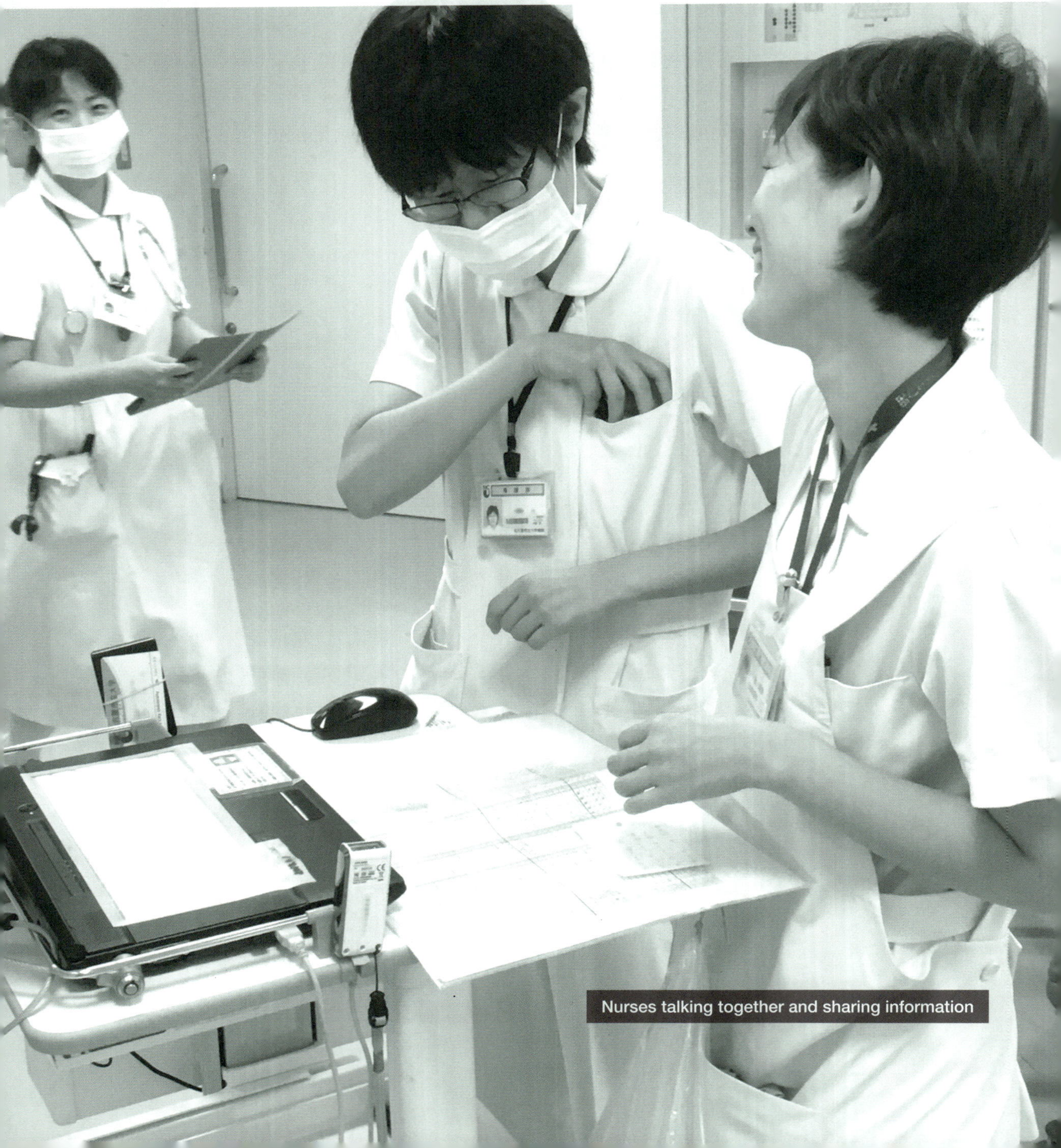

Nurses talking together and sharing information

患者の抱えている症状は、始まったばかりのものもあれば、ずっと長く続いてきたものもあります。適切な治療を行うために、症状の持続時間を尋ね、その答えを正確に聞き取りましょう。英語を話すときはゆっくりでもいいのです。必要な情報をはっきりと伝えることが大切です。

Dialog

B-02

Nurse

Patient

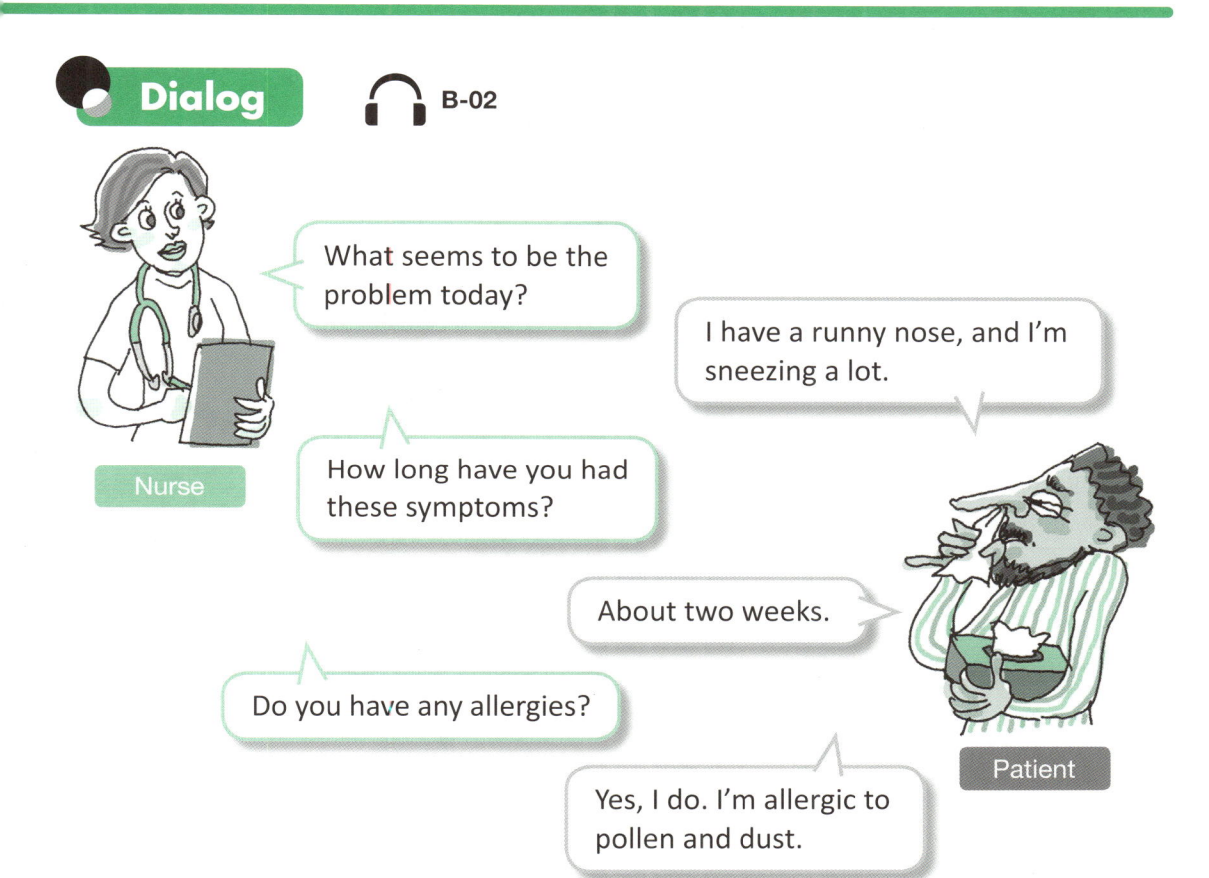

Nurse: What seems to be the problem today?

Patient: I have a runny nose, and I'm sneezing a lot.

Nurse: How long have you had these symptoms?

Patient: About two weeks.

Nurse: Do you have any allergies?

Patient: Yes, I do. I'm allergic to pollen and dust.

Vocabulary

sneeze /sniːz/ くしゃみをする　**allergy** /ǽlərdʒi/ アレルギー　**pollen** /pá(ː)lən/ 花粉

B-03

Variations

- 痛みはどれくらい続いていますか。　**How long have you had the pain?**
- 痛みを感じ始めたのはいつですか。　**When did you start to feel the pain?**
- 症状はいつ始まりましたか。　**When did your symptoms start?**

Vocabulary Building

B-04

症状 3（全体症状）

症状名と一致するイラストを選び、その記号を　　　に入れましょう。また、症状名を日本語で空欄に書きましょう。

1	bleeding		
2	fever		
3	rash		
4	inflammation		
5	anemia		
6	allergies		
7	swelling		
8	itching		
9	weight gain / loss		

a

b

c

d

e

f

g

h

i

Let's Listen

B-05 ▶ 08

A 4人の患者と看護師の会話を聞き、患者の症状についての key words を英語で書き取りましょう。また、その内容を key words から推測して日本語で書いてみましょう。

	key words	症状	症状の始まり／持続時間
1			
2			
3			
4			

B 同じ会話をもう1度聞きましょう。それぞれの患者に対する適切な症状の始まりや持続時間の尋ね方を枠内から選び、記号で答えましょう。そして意味を考えながら、暗記するまで何度も読んでみましょう。

1 ____　　2 ____　　3 ____　　4 ____

a. How long have you had that itch?
b. How long have you had these symptoms?
c. When did your symptoms start?
d. When did these symptoms start?

Vocabulary

itchy /ítʃi/ かゆい　**ointment** /ɔ́ıntmənt/ 軟膏
wheeze /(h)wiːz/ 喘鳴がする　**sluggish** /slʌ́gıʃ/ 鈍い

C ペアになって、患者と看護師のセリフを声に出して言ってみましょう。看護師役は前のページを参考にして、英語の言い回しを考えてみましょう。

1

Nurse
What is the problem today?

Patient
I feel itchy all over my body. Even when I use an ointment to relieve the itch, I sometimes wake up scratching.

Nurse
かゆみはどれくらい続いていますか。

Patient
For about a month.

2

N What is the problem today?

P It was very cold in the supermarket, but it was really hot outside. Suddenly, I began coughing. I'm wheezing. I'm having trouble breathing now.

N 症状はいつ始まりましたか。

P About 10:30 this morning.

3

N What is the problem today?

P I feel very tired and sluggish. And my throat always feels dry.

N 症状はどのくらい続いていますか。

P For a couple of months.

4

N What is the problem today?

P I sometimes feel palpitations and shortness of breath. And I feel tired all the time.

N こういう症状はいつ始まりましたか。

P About two weeks ago.

Let's Read

B-09

動物を利用した治療法の歴史は数千年にも及ぶと言われています。現在、実にさまざまな種類の動物が、さまざまな症状の患者を治療するために使われています。ナイチンゲールもその効果を認めていた治療法。実際にどんな効果があるのでしょうか。

Animal-Assisted Therapy:
Domestic animals aren't merely pets. To some, they can be healers.

When the World Trade Center collapsed on September 11, 2001, Aris, a black German shepherd and Pup Dog, a black Labrador, joined about 14 other police dogs to search for survivors. Aris and Pup Dog elevated the moods of workers by walking around the site. At meal breaks the dogs were especially popular, and the workers eagerly fed them. Each day before heading to Ground Zero, these two dogs stopped by firehouses, giving comfort to workers. What started as a recovery mission turned into a therapy mission.

Animals of all kinds, including dogs, cats, and rabbits, are being used more and more often to treat acutely and chronically ill patients. The goal is to decrease stress and improve patients' physical condition and attitudes. The therapy uses animals that have been evaluated for temperament, are in good health, and have undergone extensive training.

In 1859, Florence Nightingale wrote: "A small pet animal is often an excellent companion for the sick, particularly for long chronic cases." She recommended that patients care for animals, stating that this was beneficial for recovery. Animals have been used in various cultures for therapeutic purposes for thousands of years.

Vocabulary

4 **elevate** …を陽気にする
7 **Ground Zero** グラウンドゼロ（2001年にアメリカで起こった同時多発テロ事件で崩落した世界貿易センタービルの跡地）
14 **evaluate** …を評価する
15 **temperament** 気質
undergo …を経験する
16 **extensive** 広範囲の
20 **beneficial** 役に立つ
21 **therapeutic** 治療の

PHYSIOLOGICAL BENEFITS

Most studies that support the physiological benefits of animal-assisted therapy indicate an increase in relaxation, as evidenced by reductions in blood pressure and heart rate. Case reports of animals used in rehabilitation programs show other physical benefits. For example, a patient who has had a stroke might gain strength and muscle conditioning by using a wrist weight to increase resistance while brushing an animal.

EMOTIONAL BENEFITS

Some studies have shown psychological benefits as well: significant improvements in social functioning, impulse control, and daily activities; decreased stress levels and increased feelings of self-worth. Prisons use animal interaction as a behavior-modification tool and as a reward for good behavior.

Animal-assisted therapy is done one-on-one, and should be performed by a trained practitioner. Animals must be clean, currently vaccinated, and free of disease and parasites. The key to a safe animal-assisted therapy program is to have consistent evaluation and training guidelines for the handlers and animals as well as for the nurses.

Vocabulary

24 **physiological** 生理的な
29 **conditioning** 調整力
34 **impulse** 衝動
35 **self-worth** 自尊心
36 **interaction** 相互作用
modification 変更
40 **vaccinate** …に予防接種をする
parasite 寄生虫

A 本文の内容と一致するものに T (True) を、一致しないものには F (False) を書きましょう。

1. (　　) Aris と Pup Dog は被災地で生存者の捜索に当たった。
2. (　　) 2 匹は現地の作業員の心をいやすために派遣された。
3. (　　) 2 匹は食事も取らずに働いたことで作業員たちの記憶に残った。
4. (　　) アニマル・セラピーの目的は、患者の症状を肉体的にも精神的にも改善することである。
5. (　　) アニマル・セラピーで使われる動物は、患者との相性を優先して決定される。
6. (　　) ナイチンゲールによると、長期間病気を患っている人ほどアニマル・セラピーの効果は期待できる。

B 空欄を埋めて、アニマル・セラピーで期待できる効果を表にまとめましょう。

効果の種類	効果の例
生理的効果	■ (　　　　　　) を高める。具体的には、(　　　　　　) と (　　　　　　) が低下する。 ■ (　　　　　　) と (　　　　　　) が得られる。
(　　　　　　) 効果	■ (　　　　　　) (　　　　　　) (　　　　　　) の点で改善がみられる。 ■ ストレスが軽減する。 ■ (　　　　　　) を高める。

Let's Write

質問に答えてみましょう。

Q. Do you think animal-assisted therapy is effective? Why or why not?

A. ______________________________

____

UNIT 10

I'm going to take a blood sample.

検査の手順を説明しましょう

A nurse preparing a syringe for an MRI test

病気やけがの治療を受ける外国人患者の気持ちを考えてみましょう。「痛いだろうか」「治るだろうか」「どんな治療だろうか」「どれくらい時間がかかるのだろうか」、などと心配しているに違いありません。英語できちんと説明して、その不安を和らげてあげましょう。

Dialog

B-10

Nurse: We are going to take a blood sample. Please hold out your arm.

Patient: Like this?

Nurse: Good. Make a tight fist. It will prick a little.

Patient: OK.

Nurse: We're finished now. You can relax now. Press this cotton against the spot for about five minutes.

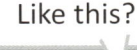

Nurse

Patient

Vocabulary

fist /fɪst/ 握りこぶし　**prick** /prɪk/ チクッと痛む　**IV drip** = intravenous drip /ìntrəvíːnəs drɪp/ 点滴

B-11

Variations

- 点滴／注射をします。　We're going to give you an IV drip / an injection.
- 検査室へ行ってください。　Please go to the examination room.
- 検査室の前でお待ちください。　Please wait in front of the examination room.
- 痛くない検査ですよ。　It isn't a painful examination.
- 横に／うつぶせになってください。　Please lie on your side / stomach.
- 20分で終わります。　It'll be over in 20 minutes.

Vocabulary Building

B-12

検査・処置

検査と処置に関する用語と一致するイラストを選び、その記号を　　に入れましょう。また、用語を日本語で空欄に書きましょう。

1	injection / shot		
2	X-ray		
3	urine test		
4	gastroscopy		
5	blood test		
6	mammogram		
7	stool test		
8	pregnancy test		
9	intravenous drip		
10	electrocardiogram		

a

b

c

d

e

f

g

h

i
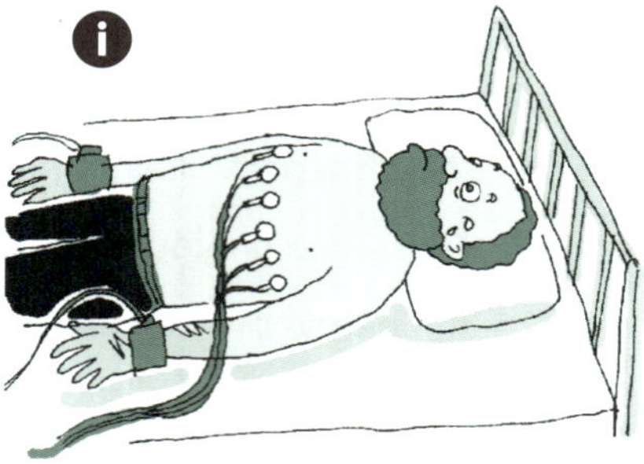

j

Let's Listen

B-13 ▶ 16

A 4人の患者と看護師の会話を聞き、患者の質問の key words を英語で書き取りましょう。また、その内容を key words から推測して日本語で書いてみましょう。

	key words	質問
1		
2		
3		
4		

B 同じ会話をもう1度聞きましょう。それぞれの患者への適切な検査の説明を枠内から選び、記号で答えましょう。そして意味を考えながら、暗記するまで何度も読んでみましょう。

1 ____ 2 ____ 3 ____ 4 ____

a. We have to give you an injection to stop your stomach from moving.
b. We're going to give you an IV drip. It contains some nutrients.
c. As the doctor said, you need to have a stomach X-ray.
d. We're going to do a urine test. Please pass some urine into the cup.

Vocabulary

nutrient /njúːtriənt/ 栄養素

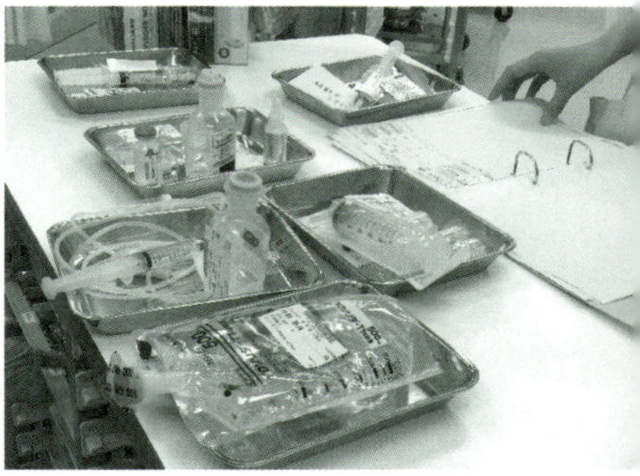

C ペアになって、患者と看護師のセリフを声に出して言ってみましょう。看護師役は前のページを参考にして、英語の言い回しを考えてみましょう。

1

Nurse
点滴をします。栄養剤が入っています。

Patient
How long will it take?

Nurse
It'll take about two hours. Please go to the restroom before we start. Let me know if you feel sick.

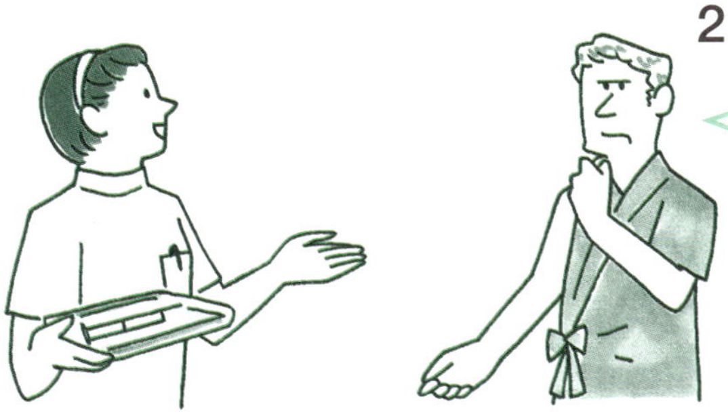

2

N 胃の動きを止めるために注射をします。

P Where are you going to give me the injection?

N On the shoulder. Please expose your shoulder. After the injection, press this cotton pad against your skin, tightly, for about five minutes.

3

N 尿検査をします。カップに尿を入れてください。

P How much do you need?

N Please fill one-third of the cup. Use the bathroom next to the examination room.

4

N 医師が言ったように、胃のエックス線検査が必要です。

P Is it painful?

N No, it isn't a painful test. On the day of the test, do not eat food or drink anything. Please be at the X-ray room by 9:00 a.m.

Let's Read

B-17

人の体には、夜は寝て昼間は起きているというリズムが組み込まれています。夜間勤務には悪影響もいくつかありますが、利点も少しあります。生物の体のリズムに影響を与えるツァイトゲーバーを利用して、夜勤を乗り切る方法を知りましょう。

Surviving the Night Shift: Making *Zeitgeber* work for you.

Humans are programmed both internally and externally to be asleep at night and awake during the day. Night shifts disturb this pattern, causing disruption of the circadian rhythm. Working on the night shift can cause functional, biological, and social problems. But by making adjustments, nurses can avoid many of the bad effects associated with working the night shift.

HARMFUL EFFECTS

The primary bad effects of working the night shift are sleep deprivation and mental and physical fatigue. Health problems associated with working the night shift include hypertension, high levels of glucose, gastrointestinal disorders and increased body weight. Cognitive effects of working the night shift include weak concentration, irritability and depression. In addition, most personal and business appointments must still be kept during the day, when night-shift workers should be asleep.

BENEFITS

There are advantages to working nights, including higher pay, an easier commute and uncrowded stores.

COPING STRATEGIES

Choose your *Zeitgeber* wisely! Activity, food, and light all

Vocabulary

title **night shift** 夜間勤務
Zeitgeber ツァイトゲーバー（体内時計の周期に影響を与える外的因子）
3 **disruption** 混乱
circadian 24時間（周期）の
5 **biological** 生物学的な
adjustment 調整
10 **deprivation** 欠乏
12 **glucose** ブドウ糖
gastrointestinal disorder 胃腸障害
13 **cognitive** 認知に関する
14 **irritability** 短気
20 **commute** 通勤

serve as *Zeitgeber*. In fact, a *Zeitgeber* can be anything that cues your body to the day's (or night's) rhythm. Light is by far the most powerful *Zeitgeber*. Body temperature, part of the circadian rhythm, is also important. Here are some tips to making *Zeitgeber* work for you in your home:

1. Wear dark sunglasses on your way home from work.
2. Give yourself time to unwind with relaxing activities such as reading or listening to music.
3. Keep a sleep diary in order to find your "personal best" time to sleep.
4. Defend your sleep. Let family and friends know your "Do Not Disturb" hours.
5. Keep your bedroom cool and quiet.
6. Eat lightly before sleeping.
7. Avoid alcohol and self-medication.

Stimulation can keep you awake. When you feel sleepy on your shift, move around, take a walk, or use a cool, damp washcloth on your face.

It is important to individualize your approach to adapting to the night shift. Although no one can adjust completely, if you work at keeping a "regularly irregular" schedule, and experiment with what works best for you, you can maintain your health as well as your sanity while you are a night-shift nurse.

Vocabulary

24 **cue** …に合図を送る
29 **unwind** くつろぐ
39- **damp washcloth** おしぼり
41 **individualize** …を個人に合わせる
43 **regularly** 規則正しく
irregular 不規則な
45 **sanity** 健全さ

A 以下の事柄が夜間勤務による悪影響なのか利点なのかを分類して、その意味を日本語で次のページの表に書きましょう。

a. easier commute	**b.** increased body weight	**c.** higher pay
d. hypertension	**e.** uncrowded stores	**f.** gastrointestinal disorder
g. sleep deprivation	**h.** weak concentration	

悪影響		利点	
f	胃腸障害	e	空いた店で買い物

B 本文には、ツァイトゲーバーを上手に利用して夜勤を乗り切る方法が 7 つ書いてあります。次の絵は何番の方法なのかを考えて番号を入れましょう。

a ☐

b ☐

c ☐

d ☐

e ☐

f ☐

g ☐

Let's Write

質問に答えてみましょう。

Q. What *zeitgebers* will work well for you? (ex. activity, food, and light) Why?

A. ______________________________

____

UNIT 11

Let me take your vital signs.

入院患者との会話を学びましょう

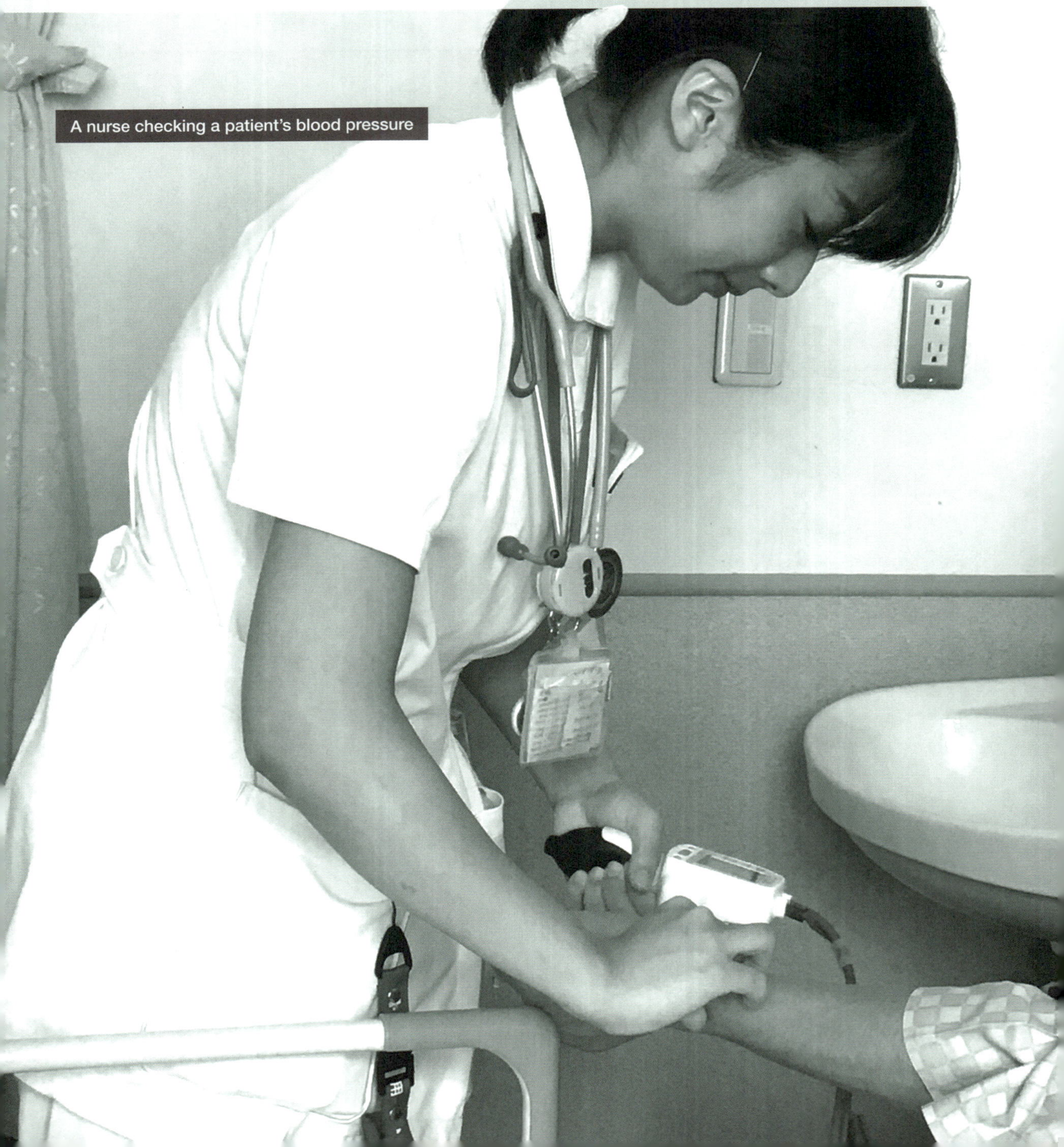

A nurse checking a patient's blood pressure

看護師は入院した外国人患者と毎日言葉を交わすことになります。バイタルサインを調べるのは毎朝の大切な仕事です。「体温を測る」「血圧を測る」「脈拍を測る」などを英語でどう表現するかを覚えて、てきぱきと仕事を進められるようにしましょう。

Dialog

B-18

Nurse: I'd like to take your temperature, pulse and blood pressure. Please place this thermometer under your arm.

Patient: OK.

Nurse: It's 36.5 degrees. Let's check your pulse now. Please extend your wrist.

Patient: Yes.

Nurse: Your pulse is 80 beats per minute. Let me check your blood pressure. Please extend your right arm. It's 130 over 85. That's normal.

Patient: Thank you.

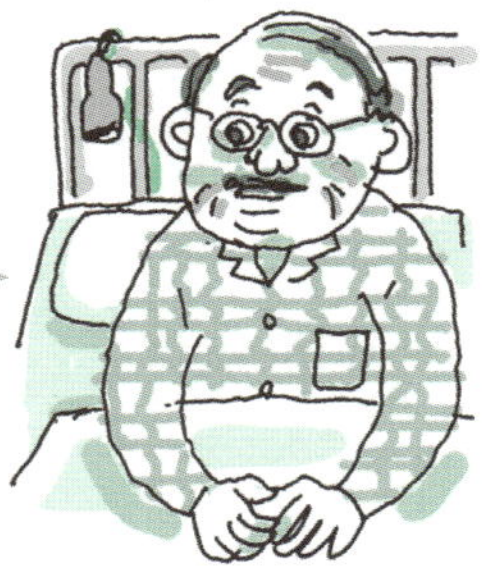

Vocabulary

thermometer /θərmá(:)mətər/ 体温計

B-19

Variations

- 体温を測りましょう。 **Let me take your temperature.**
- 脈拍を測ります。 **I have to take your pulse.**
- 血圧を測ります。 **I'd like to take your blood pressure.**

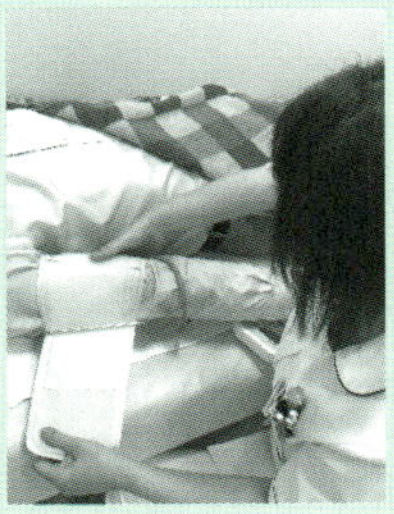

Vocabulary Building

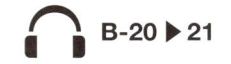

B-20 ▶ 21

専門用語を解読 1

pneumonoultramicroscopicsilicovolcanoconiosis って何？

答えは珪性肺塵症（けいせいはいじんしょう）。「細かい石の粉塵を吸い込んで起こる肺の病気」のことです。この単語は英語で最も長い単語の一つと言われますが、読むときは pneumono(肺)-ultra(極端)-microscopic(微細)-silico(ケイ素)-volcano(火山)-coni(塵)-osis(病状)のように構成要素ごとに区切ります。専門用語は接頭辞・語根・接尾辞などがパズルのように組み合わさっているので、それぞれのパーツを覚えていくと効率よくたくさん覚えることができます。

A Sleep Apnea Syndrome（睡眠時無呼吸症候群）は pnea（呼吸）に由来する用語です。pnea に接頭辞がつくと意味はどのように変わるでしょうか。例にならって Hints を参考に、正しい意味を選んで（　　）に入れましょう。

例）apnea （　無呼吸　）
1. eupnea （　　）
2. dyspnea （　　）
3. hypopnea （　　）
4. orthopnea （　　）
5. hyperpnea （　　）

例）無呼吸
過呼吸
起座呼吸
呼吸困難
呼吸低下
正常呼吸

Hints

a- (without)
eu- (well)
dys- (difficult)
hypo- (under)
ortho- (upright)
hyper- (over)

B 例にならって語群 A（接頭辞）と語群 B を組み合わせ、日本語と同じ意味になる単語を作りましょう。

例）術後 postsurgery
1. 抗体 ______
2. 紫外線 ______
3. 移植 ______
4. 静脈内の ______
5. 半昏睡 ______
6. 脱水症 ______
7. 内視鏡 ______
8. 表皮 ______
9. 高血圧症 ______
10. 栄養失調 ______

語群 A	語群 B
例）post- (after)	例）surgery
anti- (against)	scope
de- (away)	nutrition
endo- (within)	venous
epi- (upon)	tension
hyper- (over)	body
intra- (inside)	dermis
mal- (bad)	hydration
semi- (half)	plant
trans- (across)	violet
ultra- (beyond)	coma

Let's Listen

B-22 ▶ 25

A 4 人の患者と看護師の会話を聞き、患者の質問の key words を英語で書き取りましょう。また、その内容を key words から推測して日本語で書いてみましょう。

	key words	質　問
1		
2		
3		
4		

B 同じ会話をもう 1 度聞きましょう。それぞれの患者に伝える内容を枠内から選び、記号で答えましょう。そして意味を考えながら、暗記するまで何度も読んでみましょう。

1 ＿＿＿　　2 ＿＿＿　　3 ＿＿＿　　4 ＿＿＿

a. You can use the bath between 10:00 a.m. and 4:00 p.m.
b. Meal times are 7:30 a.m., noon and 6:00 p.m.
c. Let's change your position to prevent bedsores.
d. It's time to take your medicine. You'll have a different kind of medicine this time.

Vocabulary

bedsores /bédsɔ̀ːrz/ 床ずれ

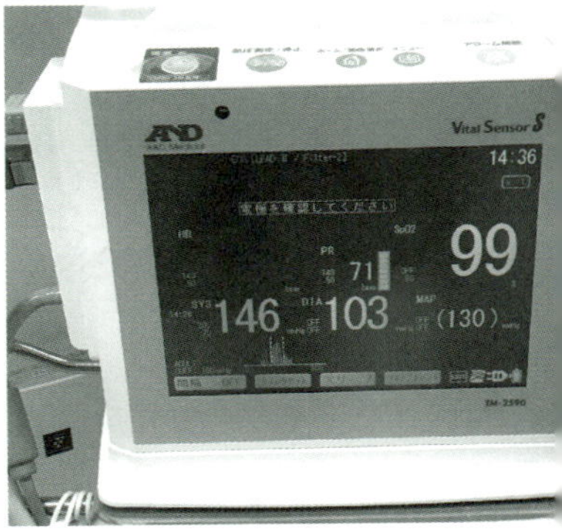

C ペアになって、患者と看護師のセリフを声に出して言ってみましょう。看護師役は前のページを参考にして、英語の言い回しを考えてみましょう。

1

Nurse
食事の時間は７時半、正午と６時です。

Patient
May I have tea?

Nurse
Sure. I'll bring you some tea.

2

N お風呂は午前 10 時から午後４時まで使えます。

P How can I request to take a bath?

N Please write your name on the list in the bathroom.

3

N お薬の時間です。今回はお薬の種類が変わりますよ。

P Is this the medicine the doctor was talking about?

N Yes, it is.

4

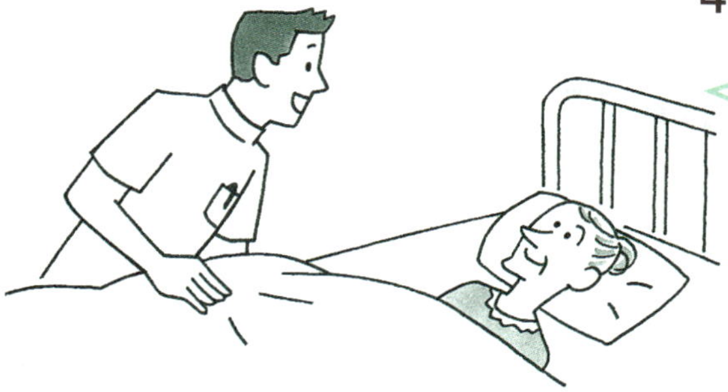

N 床ずれができないように体位を変えましょう。

P Will you help me to change my position?

N Of course.

Let's Read

B-26

"A Smart Doctor Listens to the Nurses." という言葉は、医師である筆者が、看護師である母親からもらった、貴重な助言です。患者に常に寄り添っている看護師だからこそ持ち得る情報の重要性を認識することが大切です。

A Smart Doctor Listens to the Nurses

I was in the hall outside a patient's room with a group of new interns and residents. As usual, they had all made rounds first thing in the morning, checked on new lab results, examined their patients, and were now ready to report everything to me, the attending. And, as usual, these bright, eager residents, though anxious to do a good job, hadn't thought to talk with the nurses taking care of their patients.

I patiently started my spiel. "You dart in and dart out. Your impression of your patient is like a snapshot. Your patient's nurse has been here for 12 hours. Her impression is like a video. You can't tell me you've made rounds unless you can tell me the nurse's name and what she has to say." I continued, "Say this to the nurse, each time: How are things? Anything you're concerned about? Anything you think I should know? Any orders you think I might want to change?" My residents seemed surprised by this notion.

I'm the daughter of a nurse. When I went off to medical school, Mom told me, "I don't often give unasked-for advice. But I will tell you this—a smart doctor listens to the nurses." That advice has helped me for the past 25 years as I practiced pediatrics.

My mother grew up on a small farm. Her family was poor, so she did factory work to save for nursing school. But her

Vocabulary

2 **intern** 医学研修生
resident 研修医
5 **attending** 指導医、担当医
8 **spiel** 熱弁、大げさな演説
dart 駆ける
9 **snapshot** スナップ写真
18 **unasked-for** おせっかいな

brother needed surgery, so she used all her money for that. An anonymous donor heard the story and paid her nursing school fees. She loved nursing school, and became a hospital nurse. When I was a kid, I was fascinated by her stories. When I was in high school, she was head nurse in the local ED. When I was in college, and doing premed observations with local physicians, they always suggested that I could learn more from watching my mom than anyone else. "She's seen it all," they said.

So when I went off to medical school (at the same school my mother attended), I was always conscious that I was walking the same halls she had trod 30 years earlier. When I didn't know what to do, asking the nurse would put me on the right track. And when I spent my first week in practice as a pediatrician, I wished she were my office nurse, to help me with all of the real world issues I hadn't yet learned.

So here I am, after 10 years as an office pediatrician, four as a hospital administrator, and 12 as a pediatric hospitalist. Last night I took care of a patient with critical hypocalcemia, discovered only because a clever nurse noticed some subtle muscle twitching in the middle of the night. She was sure something wasn't right, even though the patient said he felt just fine. She called me, and I listened. A smart doctor listens to the nurses.

Vocabulary

25 **anonymous** 匿名の
donor 寄贈者
27 **fascinate** …を魅了する
35 **tread** …を歩く（trod = 過去分詞）
41 **administrator** 管理者
hospitalist 総合診察医
42 **hypocalcemia** 低カルシウム血症
43 **subtle** 微妙な
44 **twitching** けいれん

A 第１・第２段落には、病院において立場の違うドクターが登場します。medical school を卒業し、研修を積むにつれて何と呼ばれるでしょうか。下線部に英語で答えましょう。

Graduate from medical school → ________ → ________ → ________ (doctor)

B 下の表の 6 つの質問に英語で答えましょう。

Question	Answer
1. What did the new residents not think of?	
2. According to the writer, what is the resident's impression of their patients like? Also what is the nurse's impression like?	
3. What was the advice of the writer's mother?	
4. What kind of nurse was the writer's mother?	
5. When the writer started working as a pediatrician, what did she wish?	
6. Why did the writer discover that her patient had critical hypocalcemia last night?	

Let's Write

質問に答えてみましょう。

Q. Which departments of the hospital are you interested in working for? (ex. Pediatrics, Surgery, ED…) Why?

A. ______________________________

____

UNIT 12

Your surgery will be tomorrow.

手術前後の説明をしましょう

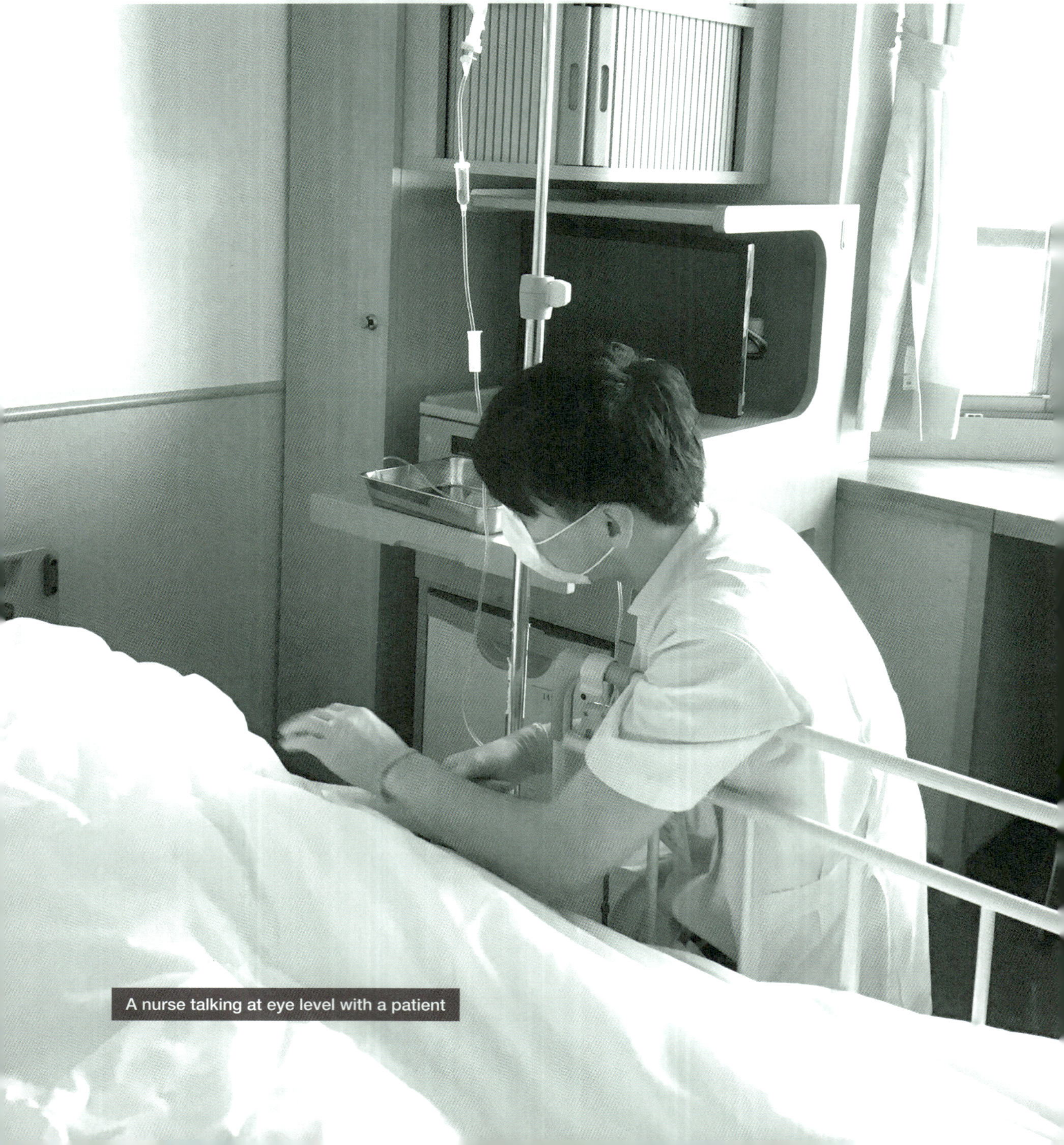

A nurse talking at eye level with a patient

手術を受けるとき、患者の不安は最高潮に達することでしょう。説明もなしに注射をされたら？　説明もなしに浣腸をされたら？　だれだってすごく嫌だと思いませんか。手術の最中はもちろん、術前術後の説明を英語できちんとできるようにしましょう。そうすることによって、患者は安心して手術が受けられて、あなたを信頼する気持ちが強くなるでしょう。

Dialog

B-27

Nurse

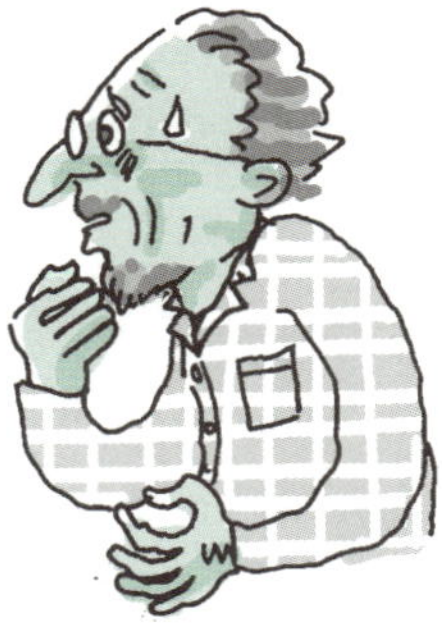

Patient

Nurse: Your surgery will be tomorrow afternoon.

Patient: I'm worried about it.

Nurse: I understand. Let me explain the pre-surgery protocol. We will give you a sleeping pill tonight. Tomorrow, you must not eat or drink anything in the morning. You'll receive an enema if necessary. You'll get an injection. Then you'll be anesthetized.

Patient: I see. How long does the operation take?

Nurse: It'll take about two hours.

Vocabulary

pre-surgery protocol /prɪsə́:rdʒ(ə)ri próutəkɑ̀(:)l/ 術前説明　**sleeping pill** /slí:pɪŋ pìl/ 睡眠薬
enema /énəmə/ 浣腸　**anesthetize** /ənésθətàɪz/ …に麻酔をかける

B-28

Variations

- 手術は明日です。　**Your operation is tomorrow.**
- 手術について少し説明します。　**I'd like to explain a little about your surgery.**
- 手術衣に着替えてください。　**Please change into your surgical gown.**

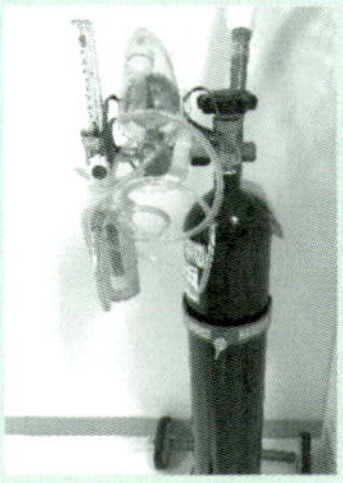

Vocabulary Building

B-29

手術・麻酔・体の痛み

手術：手術という意味の単語は2つあります。

operation	（一般的に）手術
surgery	外科手術（「手術室」という意味でも使われる）

下線部にこれらの単語を入れて読んでみましょう。

- You'll have a (an) ________________ tomorrow.
- Your ________________ will be on August 1.

麻酔：麻酔は大きく分けて、次の2種類あります。

local anesthesia	（局部麻酔）
general anesthesia	（全身麻酔）

下線部にこれらの単語を入れて読んでみましょう。

- We'll give you ________________.
- We'll use ________________.

痛み：体の痛みを表す4つの単語には次のような違いがあります。

pain	名	（肉体的）痛み、苦痛（ache より強く短い痛み）
ache	名	（体の部位の）痛み、うずき（持続的鈍痛を指し、複合語でしばしば用いられる）
	動	（体の部位が）ずきずきと痛む。痛みを感じる （hurt と違い、筋肉・背中・頭・胃などに鈍い痛みを常に感じること）
hurt	動	（体の一部が）痛む、痛い；（物が身体に）痛みを与える
sore	形	（体の一部が）けが・筋肉痛などで痛い；炎症などでひりひりする、ずきずき痛む

『ウィズダム英和辞典 第3版』（三省堂）より

痛みを表す pain、ache、hurt、sore のうち、最も適切な語を空欄に入れましょう。なお、必要に応じて正しい形に直しましょう。

1. I have a *stomach* ________________. It ________________ after I eat.
2. Where is the ________________?
3. A nasty cough can be a ________________ in the chest.
4. It ________________ when I walk and ________________ afterwards.
5. ________________ and ________________ are common symptoms of the flu.
6. I have a ________________ throat from a bad cold.

Let's Listen

B-30 ▶ 33

A 4 人の患者と看護師の会話を聞き、患者の質問の key words を英語で書き取りましょう。また、その内容を key words から推測して日本語で書いてみましょう。

	key words	質問
1		
2		
3		
4		

B 同じ会話をもう 1 度聞きましょう。それぞれの患者への適切な手術に関する説明を枠内から選び、記号で答えましょう。そして意味を考えながら、暗記するまで何度も読んでみましょう。

1 ____ 2 ____ 3 ____ 4 ____

a. You can't eat or drink anything on the day of the surgery.
b. Your lower body will be anesthetized before the operation.
c. You will be given a sleeping pill.
d. The anesthetic will wear off in about 30 minutes.

Vocabulary

gargle /gáːrg(ə)l/ うがいをする
drowsy /dráuzi/ 眠たい
conscious /kɑ́(ː)nʃəs/ 意識のある
anesthetic /æ̀nasθétɪk/ 麻酔薬
painkiller /péɪnkɪ̀lər/ 鎮痛剤

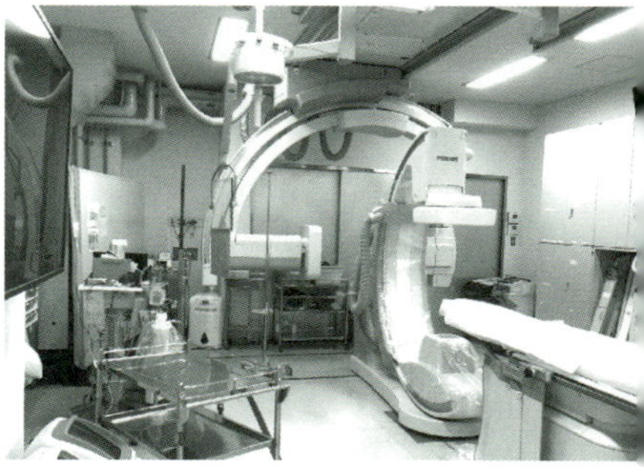

C ペアになって、患者と看護師のセリフを声に出して言ってみましょう。看護師役は前のページを参考にして、英語の言い回しを考えてみましょう。

1

Nurse
手術の日は、何も飲んだり食べたりしてはいけません。

Patient
What shall I do in case I'm very thirsty?

Nurse
You can gargle.

2

N 睡眠薬がもらえます。

P How will I feel when I wake up?

N You may feel a little drowsy.

3

N 手術の前に下半身に麻酔がかけられます。

P Will I be conscious?

N Yes, but you won't feel any pain.

4

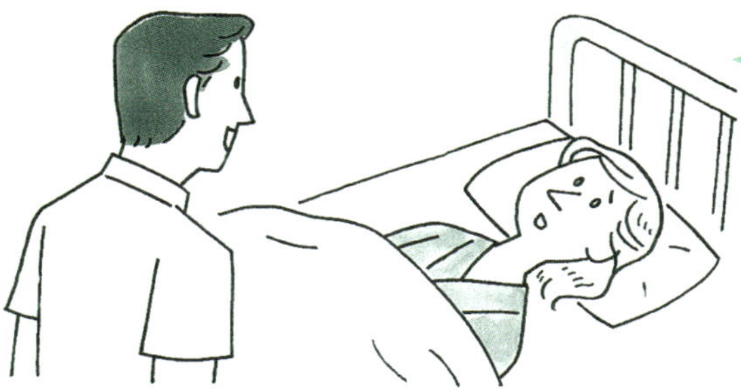

N 麻酔は 30 分ほどで切れます。

P Will I feel any pain?

N There may be a little pain, so we'll give you a painkiller.

Let's Read

B-34

どこの職場でもセクハラは起きるかもしれません。勤務中にセクハラをされたら、あなたはきっと戸惑ったり、驚いたり、悩んだりすることでしょう。どのように対処したらよいのかを学びましょう。

Sexual Harassment in the Workplace

Janet Sargent, a 32-year-old nurse, was giving a bed bath to Samuel Borsey, a 43-year-old male patient. She was making routine small talk, when he asked if she would perform oral sex. "I was angry and embarrassed," said Janet. "I treated it like a joke, finished the bath, and got out of the room as soon as I could. I just don't know what to say."

Nurses have been exposed to sexual harassment since the days of Florence Nightingale. Today, sexual harassment is still an occupational hazard. Studies show that from 33 percent to more than 50 percent of nurses have experienced some form of inappropriate sexual behavior in the workplace. The harassment can range from nonverbal to verbal communication to unwanted physical touching. Most sexual harassment is not reported because the nurse is embarrassed, fears the loss of his/her job, or thinks he/she will not be believed.

Inappropriate sexual behavior in patients leads nurses to respond with either passive avoidance or aggressive retaliation. However, an assertive approach is recommended; it will help the nurse maintain self-respect and encourage the patient to behave responsibly.

Self-awareness. Don't deny your feelings about harassment; instead, write them in a journal; talk with peers,

Vocabulary

- title **sexual harassment** 性的嫌がらせ・セクハラ
- 4 **embarrassed** 困惑した
- 7 **be exposed to** …にさらされる
- 11 **inappropriate** 不適当な
- 12 **verbal** 言葉による
- 18 **passive** 消極的な
- **avoidance** 回避
- **aggressive** 積極的な
- 19 **retaliation** 報復
- **assertive** 毅然とした
- 20 **self-respect** 自尊心
- 22 **self-awareness** 自己意識

supervisors, and psychiatric educators; and if necessary, see a professional counselor.

Defense mechanisms. Provide feedback in a non-threatening way; for example, state the facts, and use proper names for body parts. Take action by pushing away the harassing hand, and then clearly state which behaviors are unacceptable.

Assertive responses. In many cases, a statement asserting your thoughts (such as, "I feel __________ when you __________ because __________") will inform the patient that such comments or actions are inappropriate. Be sure to provide consistent verbal, non-verbal, and physical feedback.

Setting limits. Present the patient with positive behavior alternatives before detailing the negative consequences (for example, "If you stop asking me for sex, I can finish your bath and we can talk about what is bothering you. If you don't stop, however, I'll leave immediately").

Sexual harassment by patients is unacceptable and requires immediate action. Your first priority is to protect yourself, and then you should educate the harasser to prevent the inappropriate behavior from continuing. Following these guidelines will help to encourage a healthy, harassment-free work environment.

Vocabulary

24 **supervisor** 上司
26- **nonthreatening** 脅かさないような
37 **alternative** 選択肢
45 **-free** …のない

A (　　) に入る適切な単語を枠内から選び、要約文を完成させましょう。

Since the days of Florence Nightingale, sexual harassment has been an occupational (1　　　　). Studies show that nearly (2　　　　) of nurses have experienced it in the workplace. Most sexual harassment is not reported because the nurse is (3　　　　), fears losing his or her (4　　　　), or thinks he or she will not be believed. The nurse tends to (5　　　　) the harasser or retaliate against the patient.

a. half	**b.** job	**c.** hazard	**d.** upset	**e.** avoid

B セクハラに対処するには assertive approach が良いと筆者は述べており、その方法を 4 つ（a~d）具体的に示しています。それぞれの方法を示している絵を選び、記号で答えましょう。

❶ ☐

❷ ☐

❸ ☐

❹ ☐

a. self-awareness	**b.** defense mechanism
c. assertive response	**d.** setting limits

Let's Write

質問に答えてみましょう。

Q. What would you do if a patient sexually harasses you?

A. ____

____

UNIT 13

There are three kinds of medicine.

薬の説明をしましょう

Nurses preparing IV drips at a nurses station

医薬分業が進んで、薬のことは薬局の薬剤師が詳細に説明するようになってきました。それでも患者は看護師からも説明を聞きたいときがあります。何を聞いても、「薬局で聞いてください」と言われたら、患者は冷たくされたように思うでしょう。薬の簡単な説明を英語でできるようにしておくことが大切です。

Dialog

B-35

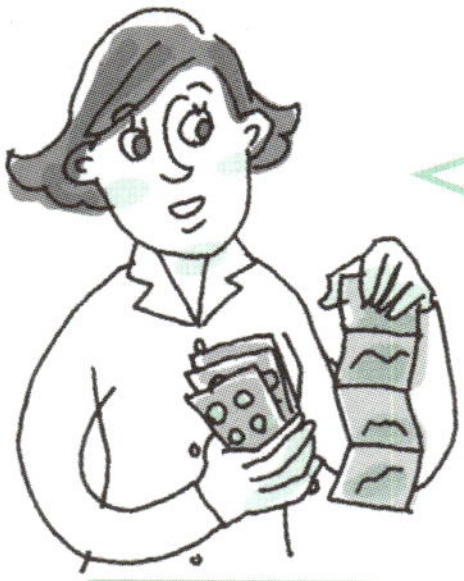

Nurse

According to the prescription, there are three kinds of medicine. Take one antibiotic every six hours. And take one tablet and one package of powder after each meal.

Are there any side effects?

Patient

To prevent you from having an upset stomach from the antibiotics, we'll give you some stomach medicine. That's the powder.

Thank you.

If you feel something is wrong, please stop taking the medicine and call the doctor.

I understand. Thank you.

Vocabulary

antibiotic /æ̀ntibaɪɑ́(ː)tɪk/ 抗生物質　**tablet** /tǽblət/ 錠剤　**powder** /páʊdər/ 粉薬
side effect /sáɪd ɪfèkt/ 副作用

B-36

Variations

- 食前に飲んでください。　**Take it before meals.**
- 食間に飲んでください。　**Take it between meals.**
- 痛くなったら飲んでください。　**Take it if you are in pain.**
- 1日3回飲んでください。　**Take it three times a day.**

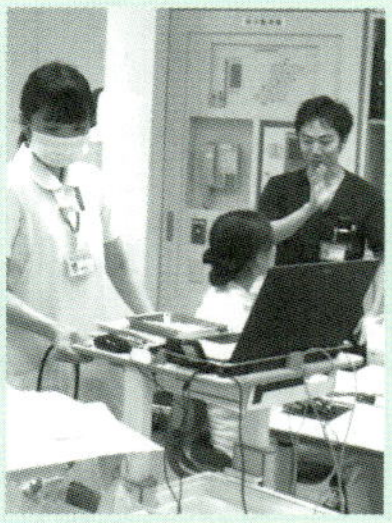

Vocabulary Building

B-37 ▶ 39

薬について

薬について大切な表現が 3 つあります。覚えておきましょう。

- **Are you allergic to any medicine?**
  薬にアレルギーはありますか。
- **Please take this prescription to an outside pharmacy.**
  この処方箋を院外薬局へ持っていってください。
- **Please ask the doctor / pharmacist.**
  医師／薬剤師に聞いてください。

A 適切な語句を枠内から選び、空欄に記号を書き入れましょう。

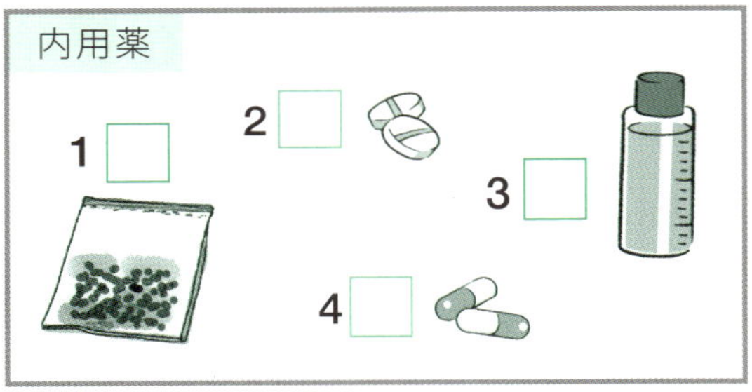

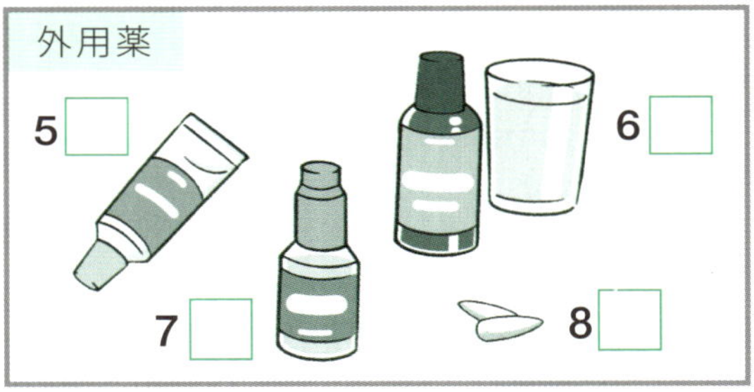

a. capsule	**b.** tablet (pill)	**c.** powder
d. liquid medicine	**e.** gargle	**f.** ointment
g. suppository	**h.** eye drops	

B 以下の症状を訴える患者にどんな薬が処方されると考えられますか。適切なものを枠内から選び、[　　] に記号で答えましょう。また、その意味を ______ に書きましょう。

1. "I have bacterial pneumonia." [　　] ______
2. "I have been constipated for about a week." [　　] ______
3. "I'm irritable and can't sleep at night." [　　] ______
4. "I have a severe headache." [　　] ______

a. painkiller　**b.** tranquilizer　**c.** antibiotics　**d.** laxative

Let's Listen

B-40 ▶ 43

A 4人の患者と看護師の会話を聞き、患者の質問の key words を英語で書き取りましょう。また、その内容を key words から推測して日本語で書いてみましょう。

	key words	質問
1		
2		
3		
4		

B 同じ会話をもう1度聞きましょう。それぞれの患者への薬の説明を枠内から選び、記号で答えましょう。そして意味を考えながら、暗記するまで何度も読んでみましょう。

1 ____ 2 ____ 3 ____ 4 ____

a. This is an allergy medicine. Take two capsules after each meal.
b. This suppository is for a fever. Use it if your temperature goes over 38 degrees.
c. Please take this medicine to stop coughing. Take it between meals.
d. Here is some ointment for you. Please rub this on yourself after your bath.

Vocabulary

capsule /kǽps(ə)l/ カプセル
suppository /səpɑ́(:)zətɔ̀:ri/ 座薬
fluid /flú(:)ɪd/ 液体、水分

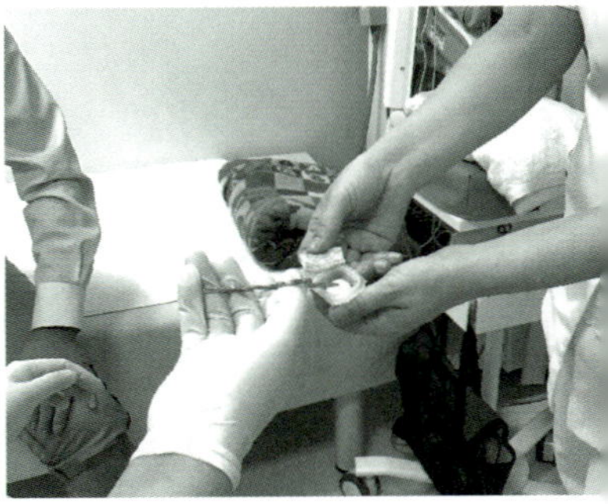

C ペアになって、患者と看護師のセリフを声に出して言ってみましょう。看護師役は前のページを参考にして、英語の言い回しを考えてみましょう。

1

Nurse
この咳止めの薬を飲んでください。
食間に飲んでくださいね。

Patient
What do you mean by "between meals"?

Nurse
It means you should take it two hours after meals.

2

N これが軟膏です。
お風呂上がりに塗ってください。

P May I use it as many times as I like?

N Just once a day is enough.

3

N アレルギーのための薬です。毎食後にカプセルを２錠飲んでください。

P Are there any side effects?

N You will feel sleepy. So you should not drive after taking this medicine.

4

N 解熱用の座薬です。
38 度以上になったら使ってください。

P What if my temperature doesn't go down?

N You can take a suppository every six hours. Be sure to drink plenty of fluids.

Let's Read

B-44

新人看護師の１年目は、不安と絶え間ない挑戦の連続でしょう。筆者は、看護師としての２日目に基本的な医療用語や考えを忘れ、尋ねられた多くの質問に間違って答えましたが、この日に “the art of saying yes” という、プロとしての重要な姿勢を学びました。それはどんなことだったのでしょうか。

The Art of Saying Yes

"I can't stand it when housekeeping leaves the trash overflowing every single night," complained the experienced nurse giving report. I looked away from my notes toward the fountain of waste—yellow isolation gowns, blood-stained blue sterile drapes, and pieces of plastic—spilling over the top of the trash can.

"How do I get them to take care of it?" I asked, eager to learn how this process worked. "Pray," she said, rolling her eyes. She gathered her pen and stethoscope along with her report sheet. "We done here? I'm exhausted," she said, leaving me with the garbage pile and no time for more questions.

Little did I know that my preceptor had witnessed the entire scene. "Do you know the number for housekeeping?" I asked. Without a word, without even a glance, she put on a pair of gloves and heaved the mound of garbage up and out of the plastic can. She tied the bag, carried the load past me down the hall, and tossed it into the dirty utility room. Returning a moment later she smiled at me and said, "No. I rarely ever call it."

Without my realizing it, my preceptor had just demonstrated the art of saying yes. There is no term for this concept in the literature. Fundamentally, this desire that

Vocabulary

9 **stethoscope** 聴診器
10 **exhausted** 疲れきった
13 **preceptor** 指導者
18 **dirty utility room** 汚物保管室

compels nurses to perform outside the realm of their title falls under Florence Nightingale's description of a "calling," a quality of those nurses who take precautions and extra steps to ensure their patients' health and safety—not because someone is looking over their shoulders, but because they feel truly satisfied when they give high-quality care.

This idea of a calling is perhaps rooted in the belief that there is no job at the bedside, whether pleasant or unpleasant, that falls outside of a nurse's capability. And while it is not a nurse's duty to attend to all of them, surprising benefits will come from the times you choose to say yes when you might just as easily have delayed, and the skill is one that can be learned and mastered early on.

I believe that the first step to expert nursing is a willingness to take on all aspects of work, and that you will be a better, more popular, and wiser nurse for it.

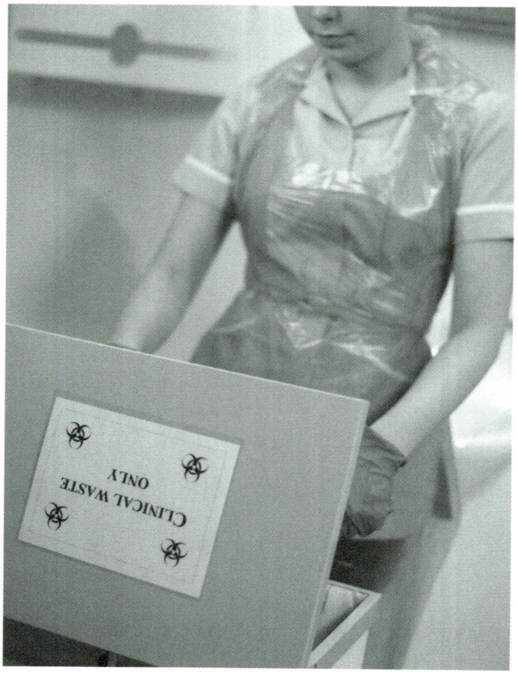

Vocabulary

24 **compel** …に強要する
realm 分野
26 **precaution** 用心

A 指導看護師が見せた “the art of saying yes” とは具体的にどの行為を指しているのでしょうか。

____

B 本文の内容と一致するものに T (True) を、一致しないものには F (False) を書きましょう。

1. (　　) 清掃スタッフは、毎日欠かさず院内のゴミをきれいに片づけていた。
2. (　　) 先輩看護師は、ゴミの山について清掃スタッフへの不平を言ったがゴミをそのままにして帰ってしまった。
3. (　　) 指導看護師は清掃スタッフに電話をかけ、早急にゴミの片づけをするように伝えた。
4. (　　) ナイチンゲールが「天職」と呼ぶ資質には、患者の健康と安全を第一に考え、義務以上の行為をすることを含んでいる。
5. (　　) 自分の義務ではないとたやすく断ってもよいことを、断らずに受け入れる選択をすると、驚くべき利益がある。
6. (　　) プロの看護への第一歩は、自分の仕事の範囲内ですべきことを確実に行うことである、と筆者は確信している。

Let's Write

質問に答えてみましょう。

Q. When you become a nurse, what kind of skills do you want to learn and master early on?

A. ______________________________

____

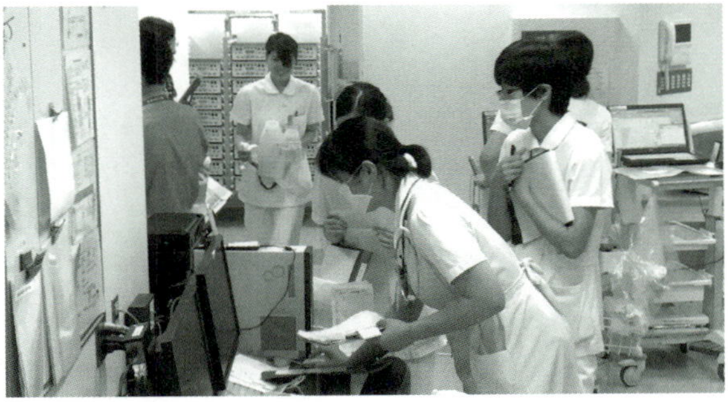

UNIT 14 Are you worried about anything?

文化の違いによる心配事を聞きましょう

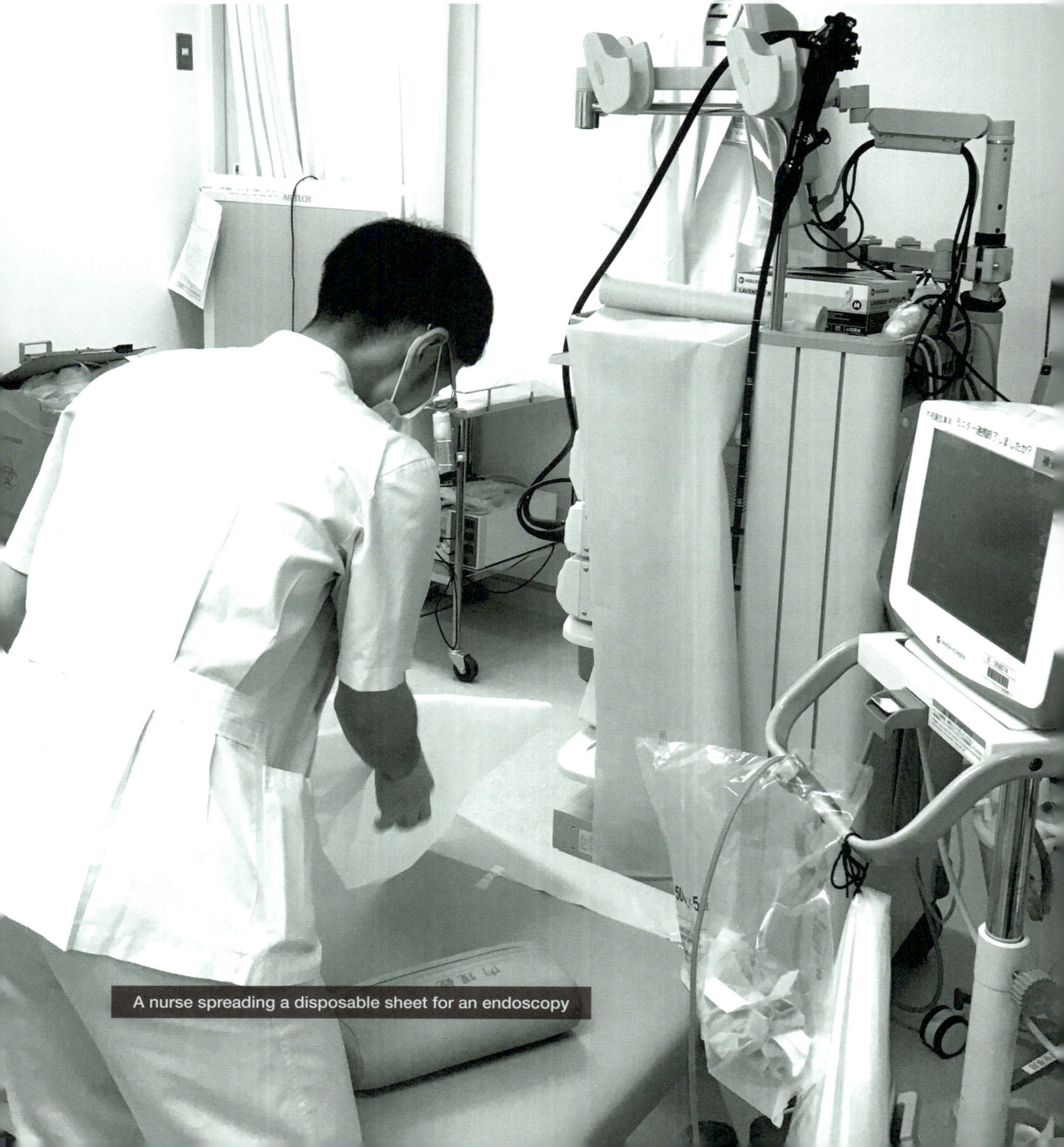

A nurse spreading a disposable sheet for an endoscopy

看護師にとって、異文化を理解することはとても大切です。文化や宗教による考え方や習慣の違いは、日本人にとって理解しがたいときがあるかもしれません。しかし、「外国人患者が自分と違う文化や習慣を持っている」ということは、人権を守るという意味からも、国際社会に生きる看護師が覚えておくべきことでしょう。

Dialog

B-45

Nurse

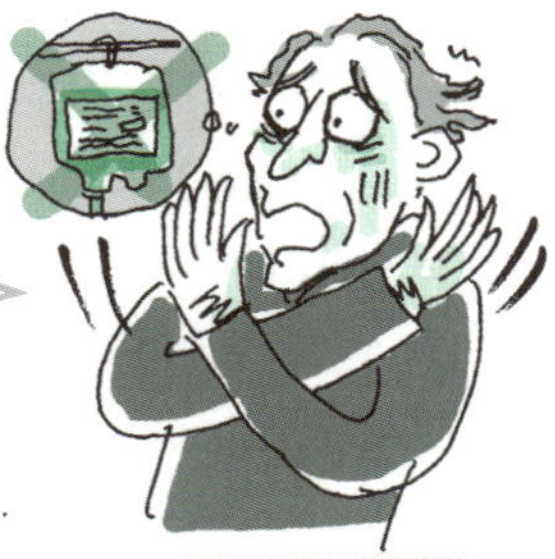

Patient

Nurse: Are you worried about anything?

Patient: The doctor told me I needed to have a heart operation. I'm really worried because he said I would need a blood transfusion.

Nurse: I understand.

Patient: I can't have a blood transfusion because of my religion. The doctor said there is a way to preserve my own blood and use it if necessary.

Nurse: We would need it for a safe operation. Will you think it over?

Patient: I'll think about it.

Vocabulary

blood transfusion /blʌ́d trænsfjúːʒ(ə)n/ 輸血 **preserve** /prɪzə́ːrv/ …を保存する
concerns /kənsə́ːrnz/ 心配事、関心事

B-46

Variations

- 何か心配事はありますか。 **Do you have any concerns?**
  Do you have any worries?

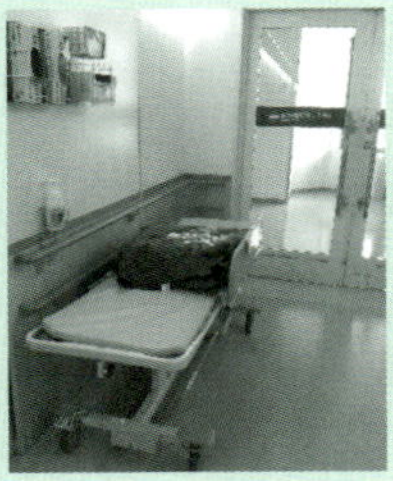

Vocabulary Building

B-47

専門用語を解読 2

leukemia、septicemia、hyperlipemia の共通点は？

共通する接尾辞 -emia は「血液の状態」を表し、それぞれ「白血病」「敗血症」「高脂血症」を意味します。語尾は用語を解読する重要な手がかりとなりますが、そのほかの構成要素 leuk- (white)、septic- (rotten)、lip- (fat) にも注目しましょう。ここでは臓器を表す語を取り上げます。

図を参考にして、それぞれの用語の意味を日本語で空欄に書きましょう。

-itis（炎症）

1. hepatitis (　　　　　　　　)

2. appendicitis (　　　　　　　　)

3. gastroenteritis (　　　　　　　　)

-algia（痛み）

4. neuralgia (　　　　　　　　)
　*neur- (nerve)

5. gastralgia (　　　　　　　　)

6. laryngalgia (　　　　　　　　)

-pathy（疾患）

7. cardiopathy (　　　　　　　　)

8. nephropathy (　　　　　　　　)

9. pancreatopathy (　　　　　　　　)

-oma（腫瘍）

10. osteoma (　　　　　　　　)

11. encephaloma (　　　　　　　　)

12. lymphoma (　　　　　　　　)

-osis（症状）

13. neurosis (　　　　　　　　)

14. osteoporosis (　　　　　　　　)
　*poro- (passage)

15. arteriosclerosis (　　　　　　　　)
　*arterio- (artery); -sclero- (hard)

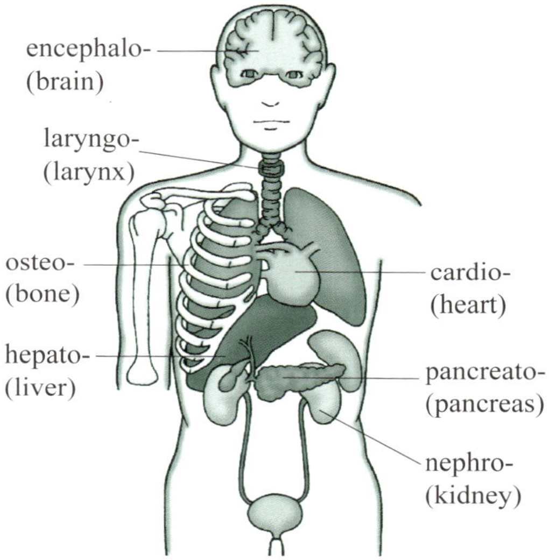

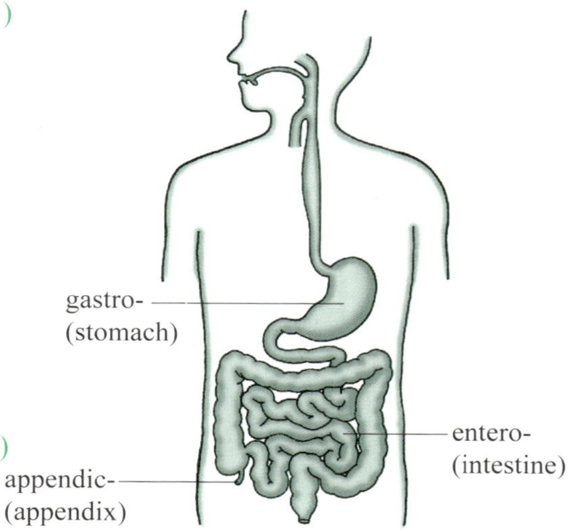

Let's Listen

B-48 ▶ 51

A 4人の患者と看護師の会話を聞き、患者の心配事についての key words を英語で書き取りましょう。また、その内容を key words から推測して日本語で書いてみましょう。

	key words	心配事
1		
2		
3		
4		

B 同じ会話をもう1度聞きましょう。それぞれの患者への適切な返事を枠内から選び、記号で答えましょう。そして意味を考えながら、暗記するまで何度も読んでみましょう。

1 ____　2 ____　3 ____　4 ____

a. I see. I'll talk about it with the nutritionist.
b. Why don't you ask your doctor about it?
c. I see. I'll tell the nutritionist about it.
d. I understand. I'll ask that a female doctor take care of you.

Vocabulary

Muslim /múzlɪm/ イスラム教徒　**unclean** /ʌ̀nklíːn/ 不浄な
nutritionist /njuːtríʃ(ə)nɪst/ 栄養士　**midwife** /mídwàɪf/ 助産師
delivery /dɪlív(ə)ri/ 出産　**Hindu** /híndu:/ ヒンドゥー教徒
prescribe /prɪskráɪb/ …を処方する

C ペアになって、患者と看護師のセリフを声に出して言ってみましょう。看護師役は前のページを参考にして、英語の言い回しを考えてみましょう。

1

Nurse
何か心配事はありますか。

Patient
I can't eat pork because I'm Muslim. Pigs are unclean creatures in our religion.

Nurse
わかりました。栄養士に伝えておきます。

2

N 何か心配事はありますか。

P I want to be examined by a female doctor. In Muslim society, a female doctor or midwife should take care of delivery.

N わかりました。女性の医師に見てもらえるようにします。

3

N 何か心配事はありますか。

P I'm not allowed to eat beef because I'm Hindu. Cows are sacred in our religion.

N わかりました。栄養士と話し合ってみます。

4

N 何か心配事はありますか。

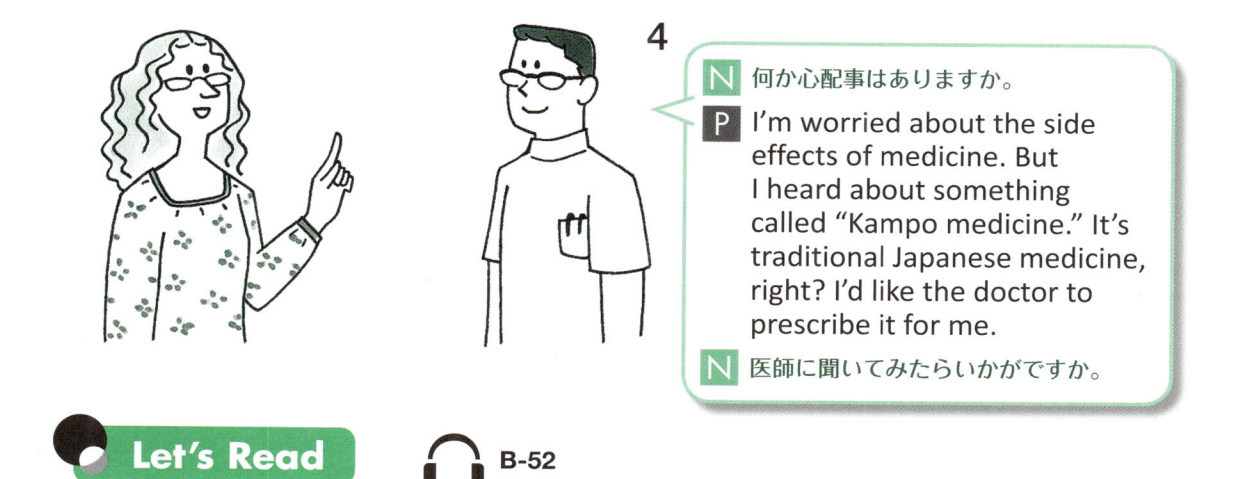

P I'm worried about the side effects of medicine. But I heard about something called "Kampo medicine." It's traditional Japanese medicine, right? I'd like the doctor to prescribe it for me.

N 医師に聞いてみたらいかがですか。

Let's Read

B-52

これは、看護実習生が患者を「個性あるひとりの人間として扱う」というシンプルなことを学んだ体験談です。舞台はナイジェリアの病院ですが、今や日本の病院にもさまざまな言語や文化を背景に持つ人々が訪れます。プロのナースとして、そのひとりひとりと向き合うためのヒントを学びましょう。

'To the Nurse Who Knows My Name . . .'

"No knowledge is wasted," goes a common saying. This is very true. A skill learned in pre-K proved useful in nursing practice many years later.

I went to a school of nursing in Nigeria, where more than 250 languages are spoken, although English is the official language. The sponsoring hospital was a place to meet patients of diverse tongues and cultures, as well as those with unfamiliar names.

I was a final-year student on my psychiatry rotation. During my first week, we admitted a patient from another country. This patient had a name that was unfamiliar to us nurses and physicians on the unit. We tried to say his name correctly.

One night, our patient had a violent episode and tried to climb out the window on the second floor. He wouldn't listen

Vocabulary

2 **pre-K** = prekindergarten

7 **diverse** 多様な

to anyone, obey any command, or answer to his name.

As a student nurse nearing graduation, I watched their efforts with keen interest, thinking of how I might help. Then I remembered that, when I'd told my grandfather, a traditional healer and herbalist, that my next rotation would be on the psychiatric floor, he advised me that if one called a mentally ill person by name, she or he would halt.

So I got the patient's chart, looked at the name again, and used my pre-K knowledge of sounding out words to figure out how to say the patient's name correctly. When I called it out, the patient stopped shaking the window to turn and look at me. I kept trying to talk to him until the security department came and got him down from the wall.

Later, I went back to that unit to ask about our patient. He'd been discharged, but had left a thank-you card for me (probably written with the help of a relative) that read, "To the nurse who knows my name . . . Thank you for calling me back!"

This experience made me determined to always try to say my patients' names correctly as I moved forward in my nursing career. I admit I haven't always been successful, but I always ask how to correctly pronounce names I'm uncertain about.

Now in the United States, the "great melting pot," it's even more important to me to be able to pronounce names correctly, and as a teacher, I encourage my students to do just that. Then it will become part of them as they rise higher in the nursing profession. Nor do I forget to remind them of the word-sounding methods of pre-K: "a says ah . . ."

Vocabulary

15 **obey** …に従う
17 **keen** 熱烈な
19 **herbalist** 薬草医
29 **discharge** …を退院させる
36 **pronounce** …を発音する
38 **melting pot** 人種のるつぼ

A 本文に出てくる pre-K knowledge とは何のことでしょうか。

B 各段落の内容に注意して、記述されている順に a ～ i の記号を並べ替えましょう。

a. 幼稚園に入る前に学んだスキルが看護実践に役立つことを学んだ。

b. 伝統的な医療者である祖父の言葉を思い出した。

c. 精神科での最終学年の実習で、なじみのない名前を持つ他国の患者を受け入れた。

d. 筆者は看護師としての仕事の中で、患者の名前をいつも正しく呼ぶ決心をした。

e. 退院した患者から、筆者への感謝のメッセージが届いていた。

f. 幼稚園前に学んだ、文字を正しく発音する方法を使って患者に呼びかけたら、患者が落ち着いた。

g. ナイジェリアの看護学校で、多様な言語や文化を持つ患者と接した。

h. 患者は、激しい症状が出て 2 階の窓によじ登ろうとし、だれの制止にも従わなかった。

i. 今は教師の立場で、患者の名前を正しく発音する重要性を看護学生に伝えている。

a → (　　) → (　　) → (　　) → (　　) → (　　) → (　　) → (　　) → i

Let's Write

質問に答えてみましょう。

Q. Do you think that "no knowledge is wasted" is true? Why or why not?

A.

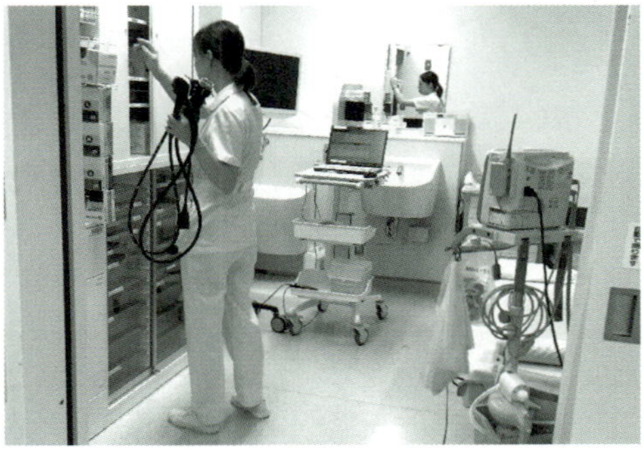

UNIT 15 It's time to be discharged.

退院後の説明をしましょう

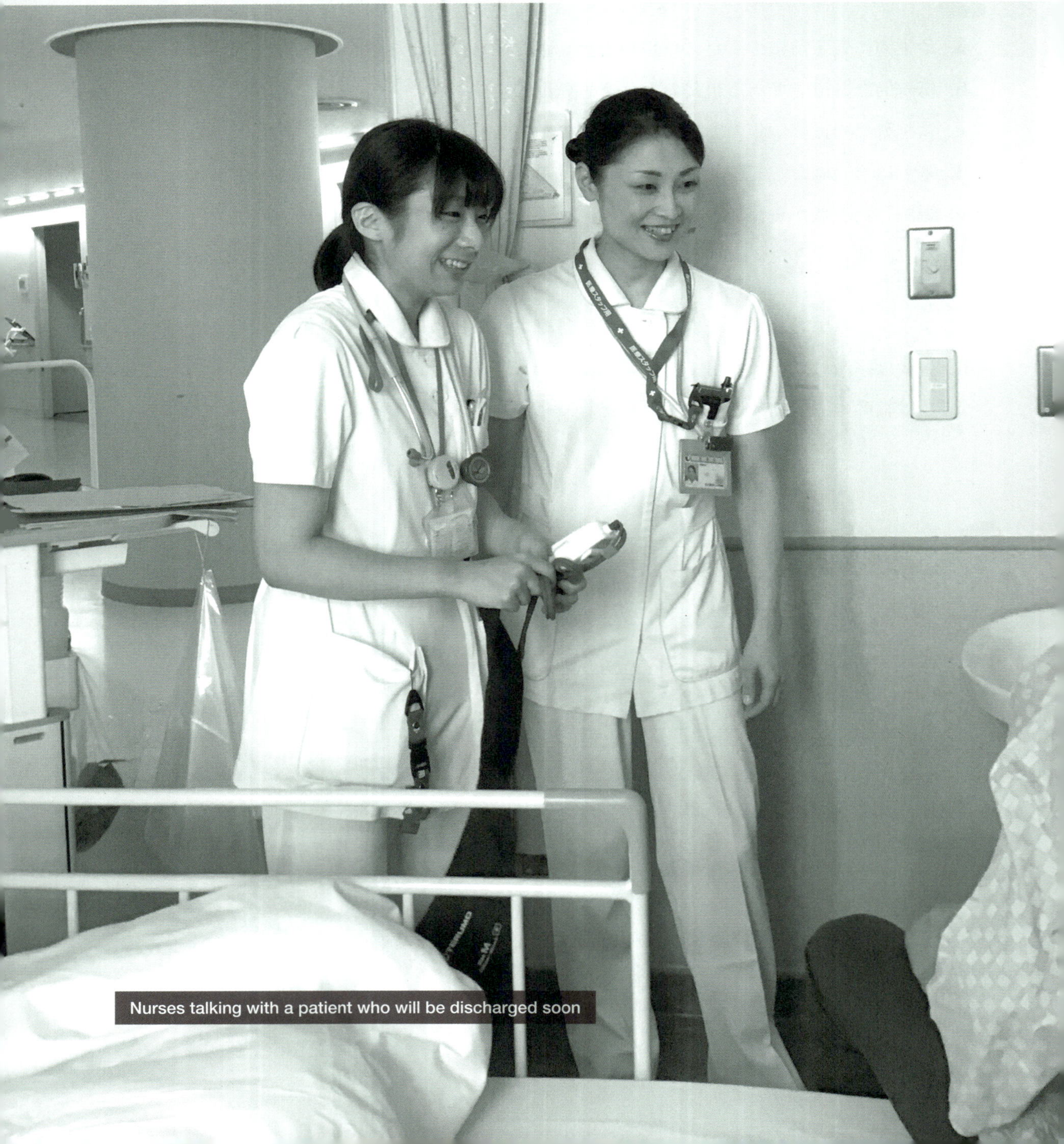

Nurses talking with a patient who will be discharged soon

退院する患者との会話を楽しみましょう。退院した後に患者が安心して生活を営めるように、退院後の生活について的確な説明を英語でできるようにしましょう。なかなか思うように英語が使えなくても、最後に「お大事に」と優しくはっきりと言ってあげること。そのたった一言の「言葉の力」を信じましょう。

Dialog

B-53

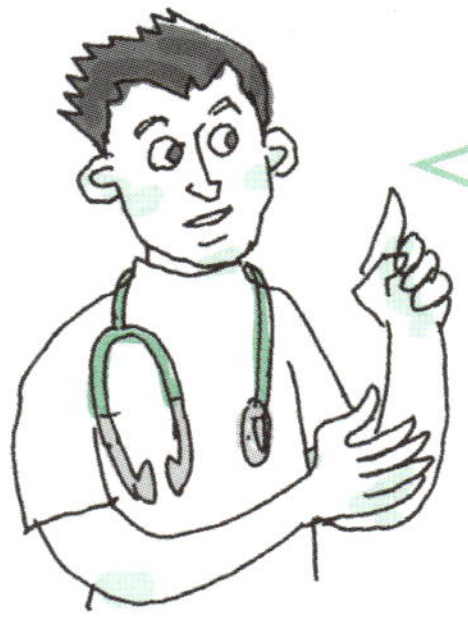

Nurse

You will be discharged the day after tomorrow.

I'm looking forward to getting back to my normal life.

Yes, but you'll still need to see your doctor as an outpatient for a while.

I see.

If you have any trouble at home, you can call us any time. Please take good care of yourself.

Patient

Thank you for everything.

Vocabulary

discharge /dɪstʃáːrdʒ/ …を退院させる　**outpatient** /áʊtpèɪʃ(ə)nt/ 外来患者

B-54

Variations

- 退院できますよ。 **You can leave the hospital.**
- 明日退院できるでしょう。 **You are scheduled to be discharged tomorrow.**

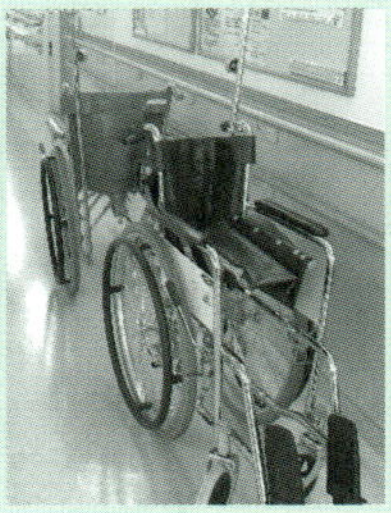

Vocabulary Building

B-55

CPR って何だろう？

Cardio**p**ulmonary **R**esuscitation /kὰɚːdioupʌ́lmənèri rɪsʌ̀sɪtéɪʃ(ə)n/（心肺蘇生法）。なるほど、書くのも話すのも略語の方が便利ですね。カルテなどで使われるたくさんの略語の中からいくつか見てみましょう。

次の略語の元になる用語は何でしょうか。例にならって、枠内から単語を選び、表にある用語を完成させましょう。

	略語	用語	意味
1	ADL	例）Activities of Daily Life	日常生活動作
2	BB	＿＿＿＿ ＿＿＿＿	清拭
3	BP	＿＿＿＿ ＿＿＿＿	血圧
4	BS	Blood ＿＿＿＿	血糖値
5	BT	＿＿＿＿ ＿＿＿＿	体温
6	CF	＿＿＿＿ ＿＿＿＿	心不全
7	CPA	＿＿＿＿ Arrest	心肺停止
8	DM	＿＿＿＿ Mellitus	糖尿病
9	HD	＿＿＿＿	血液透析
10	HR	＿＿＿＿ ＿＿＿＿	心拍数
11	P	＿＿＿＿	脈拍数
12	QOL	＿＿＿＿ of ＿＿＿＿	生活の質
13	SAT	＿＿＿＿	酸素飽和度
14	SC	＿＿＿＿ (injection)	皮下注射
15	VS	＿＿＿＿ ＿＿＿＿	生命徴候

bath	bed	blood	body	cardiac	cardiopulmonary
diabetes	failure	heart	hemodialysis		life
pressure	pulse	quality	rate	saturation	sign
subcutaneous		sugar	temperature		vital

Let's Listen

B-56 ▶ 59

A 4人の患者と看護師の会話を聞き、患者の質問の key words を英語で書き取りましょう。また、その内容を key word から推測して日本語で書いてみましょう。

	key words	質　問
1		
2		
3		
4		

B 同じ会話をもう1度聞きましょう。それぞれの患者への適切な退院後の生活に関する説明を枠内から選び、記号で答えましょう。そして意味を考えながら、暗記するまで何度も読んでみましょう。

1 ____　2 ____　3 ____　4 ____

a. I'd like to talk to you about your diet after you leave the hospital. Please follow these instructions about salt intake.

b. I'd like to talk to you about your life after you leave the hospital. Try not to do anything strenuous for a while.

c. Please see your doctor every two weeks for two months. Please go to the Outpatient Clinic.

d. You may start with some simple exercises you enjoy, such as stretching and walking.

Vocabulary

strenuous /strénjuəs/ 激しい　**diet** /dá(ɪ)ət/ （栄養面からみた）食事
intake /íntèɪk/ 摂取　**appointment** /əpɔ́ɪntmənt/ 予約

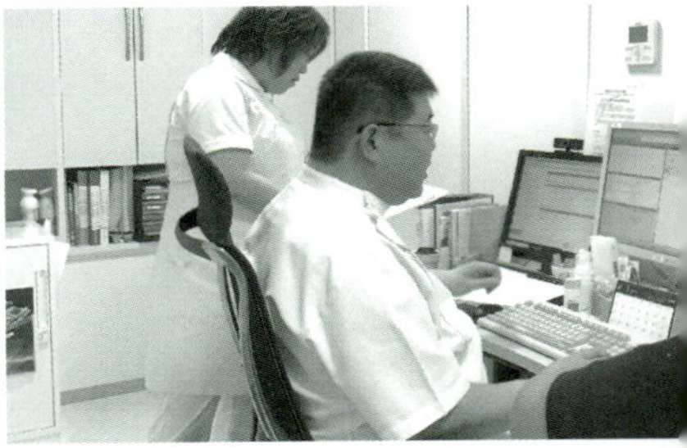

C ペアになって、患者と看護師のセリフを声に出して言ってみましょう。看護師役は前のページを参考にして、英語の言い回しを考えてみましょう。

1

Nurse
退院後の生活についてお話しします。しばらくは激しい運動をしないでください。

Patient
Is it OK to prepare meals for my family?

Nurse
If it isn't stressful work, and if it's only for a short time.

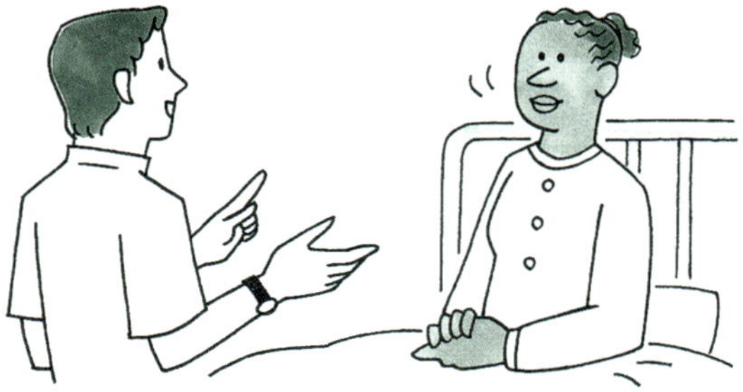

2

N 退院後の食事についてお話しします。塩分摂取は指示通りにお願いします。

P How much salt may I take?

N Less than five grams a day, which means you'll have to cut back on all foods that contain salt.

3

N ストレッチやウォーキングなど、楽しめる軽い運動から始めてください。

P How about swimming?

N Sure. I think walking in the water would be helpful.

4

N 退院後２カ月は、２週間おきに医師の診察を受けてください。外来にお越しください。

P Can I see the same doctor?

N Yes, but you'll have to make an appointment.

Let's Read

B-60

みなさんは、「国境なき医師団」を知っていますか。営利を目的としない国際的な民間援助団体で、医療援助を専門に活動を行っています。4万人近いスタッフが約70の国と地域で活動を行い、日本からも年間100人以上が派遣されています。その「国境なき医師団」に日本人看護師として参加した経験のある小林さくらさんからのメッセージです。

Overseas Volunteer

Sakura Kobayashi

June 2001 found me under the Kenyan sky. I had just joined the HIV/AIDS program team of Médecins Sans Frontières (MSF). Imagining the work ahead, I was infused with energy.

The poverty in Kenya is so serious that it formed an obstacle to our activities. Girls turn to prostitution, increasing HIV infection. Widespread HIV/AIDS has caused a shortage of hospital beds so severe that two patients have to share a bed. No matter how demanding the work gets, the hospital staff is not paid. It is difficult to break this cycle of poverty. The hospital staff is not motivated; therefore, it takes two to three months to do something that can be done in only one day in Japan. My work was by no means easy; however, I spent a worthwhile year making full use of myself every

Vocabulary

- 2- **Médecins Sans Frontières (MSF)**（フランス語）国境なき医師団
- 3 **infused with** …で満たされて
- 5 **obstacle** 障害
- **prostitution** 売春
- 8 **demanding** 厳しい
- 10 **motivate** …に意欲を起こさせる
- 13 **worthwhile** 価値のある

single day. In that year, what I learned from the Kenyan people and how I grew as a person were far more substantial than any contribution I made to the local people. They made me aware of the issues that those of us born in developed countries need to consider in the days to come.

TO BE WHAT I WANT TO BE

As I joined the Labo International Exchange Foundation at the age of 3, I was familiar with English early on in my life. As my education advanced, I became more eager to speak English, and then I had the chance to study in the United States when I was a senior in high school. Gaining confidence from this experience, I became interested in working overseas as a nurse after graduating from high school. I then thought about what I ought to do to pursue this. To study advanced medicine and to acquire nursing skills were the steps I chose to take. After taking a job at a university hospital and gaining six years' experience there, I joined MSF. By having a dream and taking the right steps, I became what I wanted to be. This is the theme of my life.

SMALL WORLD

According to one estimate, the world's existing population is 7.6 billion, and up to 2.1 billion people speak English. Supposing we can speak English, how many more friends can we make? How many countries can we enjoy traveling to? How many more people can we understand? And how much smaller can we make this big globe? I feel English is a spice that can make our lives more adventurous. I am glad to say that I was able to make my life more adventurous. Rough water makes one realize things that might not be noticed

Vocabulary

15 **substantial** 実り多い
36 **supposing** もし…ならば
39 **globe** 地球

when one is sailing on a calm ocean. In my case, thanks to the whole experience, both rough and smooth, I have continued to grow.

Q 小林さくらさんは、英語が話せるとどんなことができると考えているでしょうか。

Let's Write

質問に答えてみましょう。

Q. Are you interested in working overseas? Why or why not?

A.

小林さくらさんのプロフィール
佐賀県出身，岡山総合福祉専門学校看護科卒業，看護師として６年半勤務の後，2001 年６月から 2002 年５月まで ケニア西部・ホーマベイでの国境なき医師団の活動に参加。

Text Credits

All reading passages are abridged by Maki Inoue. (Except for Units 1, 4, 8 and 15)

pp. 10–11, Unit 1
大岡信『言葉の力』 光村図書　中学 2 年国語（国語 2）平成 13 年 2 月 5 日発行

pp. 27–28, Unit 3
Umesh, Sudha BSN, RN & Clark Angela P. PhD, RN, CS, FAAN. '*Nemaste:* I Am Mother Teresa.'
AJN, *The American Journal of Nursing*: February 2000 – Volume100 – Issue 2 – p24AAAA–24BBBB

pp. 35–36, Unit 4
Talking about your pain.: Copyright held by the National Cancer Institute (NIH)

pp. 43–44, Unit 5
Bellerose, Sally RN. Touchy-Feely Stuff.
AJN, *The American Journal of Nursing*: July 2002 – Volume 102 – Issue 7 – p. 25

pp. 51–52, Unit 6
Symanski, Mary Ellen PhD, RN. A Nurse on Mars? Why Not?
AJN, *The American Journal of Nursing*: October 2000 – Volume 100 – Issue 10 – pp. 57–61

pp. 59–60, Unit 7
Gerber, Lois MPH, BSN, RN. Nurses Know.
AJN, *The American Journal of Nursing*: January 2012 – Volume 112 – Issue 1 – p. 72

pp. 67–68, Unit 8
"Awakenings" © 1990 COLUMBIA PICTURES INDUSTRIES, INC. ALL RIGHTS RESERVED.

pp. 75–76, Unit 9
Stanley-Hermanns, Melinda MSN, RN, BC & Miller, Julie BSN, RN, CCRN. Animal-Assisted Therapy: Domestic animals aren't merely pets. To some, they can be healers.
AJN, *The American Journal of Nursing*: October 2002 – Vol. 102 Issue 10 – pp. 69–76

pp. 83–84, Unit 10
Pronitis-Ruotolo, Debra RN. Surviving the Night Shift: Making *Zeitgeber* work for you.
AJN, *The American Journal of Nursing*: July 2001 – Volume 101 – Issue 7 – pp. 63–68

pp. 91–92, Unit 11
Beach, Ann Fleming MD. A Smart Doctor Listens to the Nurses.
AJN, *The American Journal of Nursing*: April 2013 – Volume 113 – Issue 4 – p. 72

pp. 99–100, Unit 12
Zook, Ruth MEd, RN, C. Sexual Harassment in the Workplace.
AJN, *The American Journal of Nursing*: December 2000 – Volume 100 – Issue 12 – p. 24AAAA, 24CCCC

pp. 107–108, Unit 13
Anderson, Amanda MPA, MSN, RN, CCRN. The Art of Saying Yes.
AJN, *The American Journal of Nursing*: November 2016 – Volume 116 – Issue 11 – pp. 63–66

pp. 115–116, Unit 14
Kolade, Folasade MSN, RN. 'To the Nurse Who Knows My Name . . .'
AJN, *The American Journal of Nursing*: July 2012 – Volume 112 – Issue 7 – p. 72

音声ファイルの利用方法

https://ngljapan.com/lifesaver-new-audio/

A-00 のアイコンがある箇所の音声ファイルにアクセスできます。

❶ 上記 URL にアクセスまたは QR コードをスマートフォンなどのリーダーでスキャン
❷ 希望の番号をクリックして音声ファイルをダウンロードまたは再生

無料のオンライン学習ツール Quizlet でボキャビル！

https://quizlet.com/NGL_Japan/folders/lifesaver/sets

上記 URL にパソコンでアクセス、または QR コードをスマートフォンなどのリーダーでスキャンすると、Unit 2 ～ 15 の **Vocabulary Building** で取り上げている語句をクイズ形式で手軽に学習することができます。

クラス用音声 CD 有り（別売）

Lifesaver, New Edition
—Basic English in Medical Situations
話せる！ 役立つ！ 看護英語〈新版〉

2019 年 1 月 20 日　初版発行
2025 年 1 月 20 日　第 7 刷

著　者　井上真紀、佐藤利哉
発行者　松村達生
発行所　センゲージ ラーニング株式会社
〒 102-0073　東京都千代田区九段北 1-11-11　第 2 フナトビル 5 階
電話　03-3511-4392
FAX　03-3511-4391
e-mail: eltjapan@cengage.com

販売元　株式会社ネリーズ

装　　丁　有限会社ザイン
編集協力　水越由美子
本文イラスト　湊 敦子、川辺ユミ、イラストレーターズ モコ
本文デザイン　有限会社ザイン
組　　版　有限会社ザイン
印刷・製本　株式会社興陽館 印刷事業部

ISBN 978-4-86312-366-3